The
Ships
of British Columbia

An Illustrated History of the British Columbia Ferry Corporation

The Ships of British Columbia

An Illustrated History of the British Columbia Ferry Corporation

by Gary & Patricia
Bannerman

HANCOCK HOUSE PUBLISHERS LTD.

ISBN 0-88839-188-9
Copyright © 1985 BC Ferry Corporation

Edited by Jocelyn Cameron
Typeset by Hardip Johal
Design by Eugene Ristau
Production by Ristau Graphics
Printed in Canada by Friesen Printers

Published simultaneously in Canada and the United States by

HANCOCK HOUSE PUBLISHERS LTD.
19313 Zero Ave., Surrey, B.C. V3S 5J9

HANCOCK HOUSE PUBLISHERS INC.
1431 Harrison Avenue, Blaine, WA 98230

TABLE OF CONTENTS

DEDICATION

"W.A.C. used to talk about 'the jewels of the crown'—his Crown Corporations. Of all of the jewels, this was his best."
—Dave Barrett (Premier, 1972-1975)

"Among my father's considerable achievements, it became an extension of himself—the ferries more than anything else."
—Hon. William R. Bennett, P.C. (Premier, 1975-present)

The friends of his generation called him "Cec." Most who toiled with him knew him as "The Chief." He despised the widely used phrase, "The Old Man,"—the standard reference for a ship's captain—although it was uttered at all times with both respect and affection. Those of us who became his younger confidants—no matter how intimate he was in conversation—found it inconceivable and still do to speak of him as anyone other than "Mr. Bennett."

W.A.C. Bennett was genuinely mystified when the press would imply that his character was at all enigmatic or complicated. His life and philosophy were passionately   simple: devotion to family, community and basic Christian values. Distrustful of so-called "experts" and "bigness" in any form—government, business and labor—he ran British Columbia like he ran his hardware store—only the numbers were different.

Through the twenty years he served as premier, people tended to misread his good-natured sense of mischief, coupled with paternalism, as either deviousness or arrogance. When his second son Bill chose to succeed him in politics, outsiders came charging to the fore trying explain a father-son relationship they couldn't understand. Phraseology such as "nepotism, Daddy's Boy, Mini-WAC, Bennett-the-Younger, and so on, dominated the allegedly informed media.

W.A.C. Bennett was genuinely hurt by the ignorant barrage of analyses that greeted his son Bill's arrival in politics. To him, their relationship was obvious. They were two utterly stubborn, competitive, independently-minded men, who happened to be father and son, and who shared the typically masculine difficulty of expressing affection in public. They never left any doubt about it in the minds of mutual acquaintances. In a public interview with the author in 1976, W.A.C. said, "Bill is much tougher than I could ever be." Few people took notice of what he said.

It is of consummate sadness to me that W.A.C. Bennett did not live to see the $2.5 billion challenge to the wilderness called "North East Coal," using his beloved British Columbia Railway as the principal instrument of development. Or the excitement of Expo 86 and other grand Vancouver projects. These efforts are monumental and history will ultimately judge their success. What is without doubt is that had W.A.C. witnessed these events, he would effervesce with pride about his son's courage.

The following poem by Edgar A. Guest, segments of which W.A.C. Bennett quoted to the mirror every morning of his professional life, was not only his political creed, but also capsulizes what this book is all about.

IT COULDN'T BE DONE

Somebody said it couldn't be done,
But he with a chuckle replied
That, "maybe it couldn't, but he would be one
Who wouldn't say so until he had tried."
So he buckled right in with a trace of a grin
On his face. If he worried he hid it.
He started to sing as he tackled the thing
That couldn't be done, and he did it.

Somebody scoffed: "Oh, you'll never do that,
At least no one ever has done it."
So he took off his coat and he took off his hat,
And the first thing we knew he'd begun it.
With a lift of his chin and a bit of a grin
Without any doubting or quiddit
He started to sing as he tackled the thing
That couldn't be done and he did it.

There are thousands to tell you it cannot be done.
There are thousands to prophesy failure.
There are thousands to point out to you one by one
The dangers that await to assail you.
But just buckle in with a bit of a grin,
Just take off your coat and go to it;
Just start in to sing as you tackle the thing
That "cannot be done," and you'll do it.

This book is dedicated to the memory of my friend, the Honorable William Andrew Cecil Bennett (1900-1979), P.C. O.C., LL.D., D. Pol.Sc., K.St.J.

BRITISH COLUMBIA'S
PREMIER BENNETT

ACKNOWLEDGEMENTS

This book originated during a series of cruises on the BC Ferries northern service during the summer of 1983. Stuart M. Hodgson, Chairman of the Board of the British Columbia Ferry Corporation, invited my wife and I to join him and Mrs. Hodgson aboard *Queen of the North* and *Queen of Prince Rupert*. Hodgson was interested in my comments about the tourist/cruise ship aspect of the BC Ferries northern service, based on my previous publications and experience with the finest passenger ships of the world. An informal private report resulted. During our several days together, we talked about the history of the corporation he heads on behalf of the provincial government, its 25th anniversary planned for June 15, 1985, and the British Columbia co-sponsorship with Ottawa of Vancouver's Expo 86, the international exposition on transportation and communication. He proposed a book that would serve the dual role of celebrating the twenty-five years and also providing Expo 86 with a powerful illustration of British Columbia's achievements in transportation.

Over a year passed before we discussed details. Hodgson's demanding schedule and the author's other commitments, conspired to forge a lengthy delay. When we finally met, I expressed obvious concerns about the prospect of writing a "commissioned" book. I feared that the book's credibility would be destroyed by political or public relations pressures. While BC Ferries is an obvious success story, the history has not been free from error and difficulty. These matters must also be told.

It was my view that if the proper story of a shipping company and its people were told, the volatile and partisan politics of British Columbia must be minimized. In the process, it may create a deliberate disservice to the many cabinet ministers who have contributed to the company's development. Convinced that, within the bounds of diplomacy and good taste, this freedom was available, we went ahead. The Board of Directors approved the project in late 1984.

The author and publisher, David Hancock, were left with a deadline that could only be described as impossible. And impossible it would have been without the enthusiastic participation of a formidable team.

BC Ferries executives Ken Stratford and Barry Ellett put together the business details. Bill Bouchard and his talented communications staff, particularly Betty Nicholson in Victoria and Pat Stephens on the mainland, cheerfully threw open their files for exploration. In a busy public relations year marking the 25th anniversary, they frequently discovered that their most cherished photos and albums were seconded to the book project. They and their associates could not possibly have been more helpful.

I first met the BC Ferries Corporate Secretary Al Lukinuk one night in October 1984, when he picked me up at Nanaimo airport for a drive to Qualicum. After I spoke to a BC Ferries dinner, this book was announced. Lukinuk was to rejoin the project in the final stages when he, Bouchard and my good friend of many years Dave Laundy (Director of Government Information Services) helped proofread the manuscript for accuracy.

My partner, photo editor and wife, Patricia, estimates that she sorted over 20,000 photographs and drawings to determine the most suitable for this text. She enjoyed the excellent services of the Provincial Archives, the Vancouver City Archives, the Image Bank of Tourism BC, and the Vancouver Maritime Museum. Patricia met one of W.A.C. Bennett's special friends, "Big Jim" Ryan of Victoria, some of whose photographic work (including, "The Chief," of course) is included here. The photographic skills of Charles Jennings of Vancouver and Jeff Barber of Victoria are prominently featured.

Broadcasters in Western Canada have been perplexed for decades by the dominance of my radio employer, CKNW. We at the station have an obsessive compulsion to be involved in whatever is going on. Once again, I've been the beneficiary of my colleagues' assistance. Vice-president John Plul, a promoter with legendary ability, and his assistant, Jaimie Hunt, a BC Ferries buff, organized a photo contest in the spring of 1985. With the help of Mel Cooper and Joe Easingwood of CFAX in Victoria, we attracted mailbags full of listeners' BC Ferries photos. My program producer and not-so-secret-weapon, Shirley Stocker, as always, made it possible for me to pursue these other adventures.

The assistant program producer, Lorna Sandberg, was a special ally to us all. In addition to coordinating the many game players, she marched repeatedly to one of the province's finest and most frequently overlooked resources, the Vancouver Public Library. With the help of the librarians, she produced an impressive collection of research data.

Two maritime historians, writer Frank A. Clapp of Victoria and artist David O. Thorne of Tsawwassen, were generous with both their time and their knowledge. One of the most significant contributions of all came from an unlikely source, my eccentric friend, David Ingram, one of Canada's great tax minds. He taught me how to use a word processor. No one else would have had the patience.

It has been a year filled with warm memories of the Gulf Islands, Prince Rupert, the Sunshine Coast and all BC Ferries points in between; of regular weekends enjoying the hospitality of Ted Balderson and his staff at the venerable Empress Hotel; of visits to bridges, engine rooms and cafeterias of vessels both small and large and of many new friends. The courtesy and friendship of Monty and Kay Aldous in their Victoria home became a routine and pleasant interview event.

We met and talked with scores of employees, at all organizatioal levels. Space does not permit mentioning everyone. If there is a regret, it is that time did not allow meeting more. Any errors, omissions or subjective misjudgements are those of the author.

We are grateful to all of these people.

And, finally, a word about my friend Stu.

I started following the career of Stuart Hodgson in the Canadian Arctic in 1968. Late in the text of this book a number of things are said about him. If there are critics who believe I have been too generous, so be it. More has been said on my radio show and by people far more knowledgeable than I. What is certain, is that no one else other than W.A.C. Bennett himself would have been able to talk me into writing this book.

When Hodgson joined BC Ferries late in 1981, he became part of a group whose achievement has frequently attracted international attention. This book faithfully attempts to chronicle not only their history, but also the small British Columbia public who collectively and regularly complete projects of world scale. Despite occasional travelers' complaints, few in this province don't feel a personal connection with *their* ferries.

This is a story about my fellow British Columbians and *our* ships.

Gary Bannerman,
West Vancouver, B.C.
November 1, 1985

INTRODUCTION

THE SHIPS OF THE DOGWOOD

At some point during Expo 86, British Columbia ferries will transport their 200 millionth passenger. When the company celebrated its 25th anniversary on June 15, 1985, the tally had reached 187 million people and 68 million vehicles, remarkable for the company's relatively short lifespan.

The fleet of sixteen capital ships and nine smaller vessels rivals not only all the world's ferry systems, but in terms of achievement in its field, the British Columbia Ferry Corporation ranks with the most auspicious names in passenger shipping: P&O, Cunard, Holland America, et. al.

Named for the provincial flower, *The Dogwood Fleet* has the capacity to simultaneously take a small city to sea: a crew of 600 could transport over 21,000 people and more than 4,500 cars at any given moment. Over a span of ninety minutes everyone could also be fed.

It is difficult to compare the physical bulk of a ferry to any other kind of ship. Even car-carrying capacities are misleading. While American cars have become smaller, they remain substantially larger than the international average. The company's first general manager, Monty Aldous, unromantically says, "A ferry is a floating barn." When cruise ships are measured in gross registered tons, the figure calculates internal cubic capacity and revenue space: cabins, bars, dining rooms, casinos and so on. The commercial space on a ferry is insignificant. When cargo ships are listed in deadweight tons, the total reflects the actual weight of the ship when full of cargo and sitting in the water up to its Plimsoll line. Even when full of cars and trucks, a ferry still transports a tremendous amount of weightless air space.

The most suitable comparative measurement is simply the bulk of the vessel. A 20,000-ton modern cruise ship will be about 550 feet in length and 80 feet across the beam. BC Ferries' five *Cowichan Class* jumbo ships are 460 feet in length and 90 feet in width. The four stretched and lifted *Victoria Class* vessels are roughly 430 feet by 80 feet. They would equate in size to cruise ships in the 12,000 - 15,000 ton range.

Queen of Coquitlam, *and BC Ferries' four other* Cowichan-Class *vessels, are the largest double-ended ships in the world.*

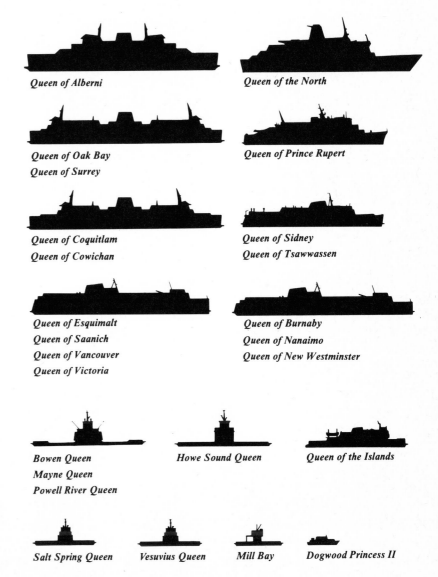

Queen of Alberni

Queen of the North

Queen of Oak Bay
Queen of Surrey

Queen of Prince Rupert

Queen of Coquitlam
Queen of Cowichan

Queen of Sidney
Queen of Tsawwassen

Queen of Esquimalt
Queen of Saanich
Queen of Vancouver
Queen of Victoria

Queen of Burnaby
Queen of Nanaimo
Queen of New Westminster

Bowen Queen
Mayne Queen
Powell River Queen

Howe Sound Queen

Queen of the Islands

Salt Spring Queen

Vesuvius Queen

Mill Bay

Dogwood Princess II

Seven ships became the back-bone of service during the 1960s, all slightly larger than the company's two originals, Queen of Sidney *and* Queen of Tsawwassen. *All of the seven were stretched with the insertion of 84-foot midsections, but four were later "lifted" by the addition of an extra car deck.* Queen of New Westminster, *along with her sisters* Queen of Nanaimo *and* Queen of Burnaby *remain in 1985 in their post-stretching, but unlifted, condition.*

The most unique of the C-Class jumbos, Queen of Alberni, *was originally designed to carry a preponderance of overheight vehicles. In 1984 a $9 million dollar expansion, maintained overheight capacity, but installed the extra car deck shown in the photo (right).*

Gross corporation sales total in excess of $120 million per annum, but expenditures substantially exceed that figure. A $40-million annual subsidy from the shareholder, the provincial government, recognizes that BC Ferries is, in fact, a marine highway—a vital communications link, subsidized from the tax base like any other roadway. The combined capital and operating accounts make it, effectively, a $150-million-a-year business with an asset base—ships and terminals—in excess of $300 million. Of the current $40 million annual subsidy, the province receives a rebate from Ottawa in the amount of about $14 million, negotiated during the mid-1970s when the federal government rid itself of historic shipping grants to companies operating on the northern west coast.

THE LARGEST IN THE WORLD?

W.A.C. Bennett was fond of saying the BC Ferry system was "the largest of its kind in the world," a phrase that amuses skeptics but has profound meaning to anyone in the shipping business. Others have flatly stated that the British Columbia service is simply, "the largest." Questioned about making that claim in 1985, the current BC Ferries Chairman, Stuart M. Hodgson, replied unequivocably, "We think it is."

Meeting with the world's largest ferry companies at the outset of the 1980s, the representative of Hong Kong's Star Ferries was asked about the state of his business. He replied that it was "terrible" since the colony's new subway system had opened. He added that the volume had dropped to 12 million passengers. The general manager of BC Ferries at the time, Charles Gallagher, exclaimed in shock, "That's about what we do!" The Hong Kong chap quickly emphasized, "That's 12 million a month."

Queen of Sidney (shown), and her identical sister Queen of Tsawwassen are still sailing 25 years after they launched BC Ferries. They remain unchanged from their 1960 birth, except for a dining room added to the main deck aft during their first few months of life.

Debating the relative size of the world's leading ferry transport firms is the kind of argument that makes cocktail parties stimulating among shipping executives. The answer is that Canada's west coast claim to having the largest is both correct and incorrect. The figures that follow are circa 1980.

It should be emphasized that British Columbia is not a nation, but a province, with a population approaching 2.8 million. Little has come from federal operating subsidies, unlike most comparisons here. Washington State's numbers include fresh water vessels and some European companies show cargo and container ships in their ferry statistics. None of this applies to British Columbia's claim. The province's substantial highways department fleet of both fresh and salt water vessels is excluded from the totals. At the end of 1985, twelve salt water vessels of the provincial highways department were being transferred to BC Ferries. Although most of these are small, there is one large ship, the former CP ferry *Princess of Vancouver*. Once completely absorbed, this will enlarge BC Ferries to 36 vessels.

No fleet can compare with the number of passengers Hong Kong ferries carry—consistently over 100 million, annually. But they transport an insignificant number of cars. BC Ferries ranks fifth, carrying 12.5 million people annually.

Europe's "Sealink" system leads the world with seventy-three vessels, but many of these are cargo, container and railway carriers in addition to cars. Despite its exclusive roll-on, roll-off car, truck and passenger service, BC Ferries still ranks fourth in the world with twenty-five vessels. Sealink, in fact, is not one ferry system, but the pooled resources of four European nations.

In number of operating routes, the Norwegian national system leads with thirty-nine. British Columbia is third at fifteen. With an

Queen of Prince Rupert *(top) originated the service north in 1966. Joined by the more spectacular* Queen of the North *in 1980, the two ferry cruise ships are regular sights in the spectacular "Inside Passage."*

One of BC Ferries most impressive engineering achievements was the "lifting" of the four Victoria-Class *ships, with the insertion of an extra car deck, expanding capacity to as many as 400 vehicles. Shown is* Queen of Victoria.

annual volume of 4.6 million vehicles carried, British Columbia trails only neighboring Washington State's 7.4 million total, almost all of which is cross-harbor commuter traffic in Seattle.

BC Ferries has no equal in the 918 route-miles of the system, and quite literally pounds all contenders into submission when this figure is converted to passenger—route-miles travelled each year. The five jumbo Cowichan-class ships are the largest double-ended ships in the world (single propeller and duplicate bridge controls at each end). The expansion of the four Victoria-class ships from an initial 105-car capacity, through sretching and lifting to a load factor of up to 400 cars, has never been duplicated.

In 1980 there were 1,044 car and passenger ferries registered around the world.

BC Ferry Corporation has the highest profile of the provincial government's transportation systems but there are many more. The BC Steamship Company transports tens of thousands between Victoria and Seattle in the summer dayliner service of historic *Princess Marguerite*. The British Columbia Railway is the north-south spine of the province. British Columbia Transit operates bus services in thirty-six separate communities, most notably the large fleets of Vancouver and Victoria. The Vancouver system also utilizes two ultra-modern harbor passenger ferries and a $1-billion rapid transit facility, due to begin its 13-mile first phase on January 1, 1986.

In cruise ship profile, Queen of the North.

Three "Powell River Class" vessels were built in 1965, as the backbone of Gulf Islands and Jervis Inlet service, for $1 million. Shown here, Bowen Queen, *and her two sister ships received new engines in 1979, providing them with almost unbelievable maneuverability.*

Vesuvius Queen *(top left)*, now in islands service, once served in the Okanagan at Kelowna. She and her 36-car identical sister Saltspring Queen *started their days crossing the Fraser River before the Deas Tunnel was built.*

Entering Horseshoe Bay is the 70-car, 330-passenger Howe Sound Queen *(bottom left).*

BC Ferries service between the mainland and the Gulf Islands was inaugurated by Queen of the Islands *(right)* in 1963. Inactive in recent times, the ship was never popular with her crews.

The Ministry of Transportation and Highways navigates a flotilla of small ferries on rivers and lakes throughout the province and even a few larger vessels serving the more remote coastal islands. One substantial ship in the fleet, the former Canadian Pacific ferry *Princess of Vancouver,* plies across the strait between Powell River and Comox. The highways department water transport activity is almost pure subsidy: annual costs of about $30 million against revenues of $4 million.

British Columbia politicians rarely fail to point out that the province is usually a solo act. A small population has used its resource and transportation muscle in a relentless challenge of the wilderness with little of the federal subsidization so frequently enjoyed on the east coast of Canada.

W.A.C. Bennett advised a 1977 Royal Commission that during the twenty years he served as premier, the British Columbia Railway had laid over one thousand miles of pioneer track. That number exceeded the new rail development in any country of the free world, and was greater than Europe and the United States combined during the same period.

"It was a truly prodigious achievement by a community of some two million people," he told the commission.

And such is also the story of BC Ferries.

The small fry of the fleet, Mill Bay *(left) and* Dogwood Princess II, *are, nevertheless, crucial to service in their route areas. The 16-car* Mill Bay—*the only vessel in the fleet without radar—plies back and forth across Brentwood Bay, near Victoria, and* Dogwood Princess II, *carrying just 38 passengers and no cars, is a water taxi service connecting Langdale with Gambier and Keats Islands.*

Repainting of the fleet in 1984 & 1985, put bold new Expo 86 insignia on all of the smokestacks, but the Dogwood emblem—British Columbia's official flower—remains the company's logo.

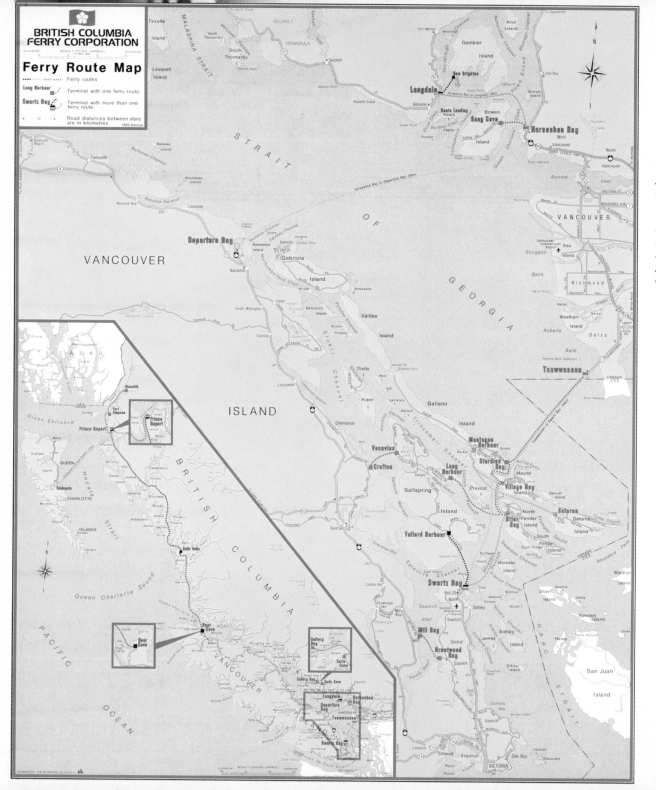

With the absorption of the provincial Highways Department's salt water vessels at the end of 1985, the route system will be expanded and revised. The current 15 routes shown cover 918 nautical miles, by far the greatest distance served by any of the world's ferry fleets.

THE LARGEST FERRY BOATS

The Scandinavians continue to establish new records for the largest individual ferry ships, some featuring extensive cruise ship amenities: dining rooms, nightclubs, gambling casinos and staterooms, along with complete duty-free shopping arcades selling everyting from groceries and liquor to hard goods. Many passengers book aboard for a return trip, and then gamble and party all night.

Likely the largest in the world are the 25,678 gross ton, 2,000-passenger, 480-car sister-ships Finlandia and Silvia Regina of Finland's Silja Line. They represent a generation of ships known in the trade as "RORO" vessels (roll on, roll off) designed to create interiors of almost perpendicular bulkheads.

Renowned Seattle naval architect, Phillip F. Spaulding, describes these vessels succinctly: "They are absolutely the ugliest ships the world has ever seen—absolutely grotesque."

SUPER, NATURAL
CHAPTER ONE

British Columbia is marketed under the banner "Super, Natural," a tribute to some of the most awesome geography on earth, spanning 366,255 square miles: a dozen major mountain ranges; 7,000 square miles of lake surface and hundreds of rivers with names that evoke images of romance and exploration—the Thompson, Liard, Fraser, Nass, Peace, Stikine and Columbia, among the many.

While the topography has frequently left visitors in speechless admiration, British Columbia offers, for those who dare try to tame her, a challenge of terrifying proportions. Sir Alexander Mackenzie battled overland from the east through savage weather with seemingly endless blind mountain canyons, until he finally reached the coast at Bella Coola in 1793. Simon Fraser took a more northerly route in 1805, exploring, in 1808, the length of the mighty river which now bears his name. When he reached the mouth of the Fraser at Musqueam, within modern Vancouver, an Indian attack forced a hasty retreat upstream.

But this is a story of maritime British Columbia, the breathtaking fjords, channels and islands that form the entire west coast of Canada—some 17,000 miles of shoreline—from Alaska to the State of Washington. The islands are yet another mountain range, or, more correctly, the weathered peaks of the Coast Range as it gives way to the Pacific Ocean. The deep water-filled trenches create the fabled *Inside Passage,* now summer home to many of the world's finest cruise ships.

Early exploration of Canada's Pacific coast remains a subject of historical controversy. Some British observers still claim that Sir Francis Drake must have spotted Vancouver Island when he sailed north in 1579, but more likely the Spaniard, Juan Perez, exploring the Queen Charlotte Islands in 1774, could best lay claim to the original sighting. It is clear, however, that the first significant landing was made by the legendary Captain James Cook in 1778, at Nootka Sound on Vancouver Island. The Cook voyage was widely reported in Europe during the next decade. Rumors told of vast fortunes to be made in the fur trade along the newly charted waters of the Pacific Northwest.

The Spanish government, which claimed the entire west coast of the Americas, expeditiously dispatched explorers to secure the

From Captain James Cook's
first arrival at Nootka Sound,
on the west coast of
Vancouver Island *(top right)*,
in 1778, an era of active
exploration was initiated.
H.M.S. Plumper *(top left)* is
shown at Port Harvey, on
Johnstone Strait. The vessels
of Captain John Meares are
shown at anchor in Nootka
Sound *(bottom left)*, as the
first boat built in the Pacific
North West—North West
America—is launched. The
period of early exploration
ended in undisputed British
sovereignty after Captain
George Vancouver met the
ships of the Spaniards,
Galiano and Valdes off Point
Grey in 1792 *(bottom right)*.

northern extremity of the hemisphere: Martinez, Narvaez, Galiano and Valdes. The British did little to respond until Martinez and Narvaez seized several ships owned by Captain John Meares at Nootka in 1789. A monumental diplomatic row ensued between the governments of Spain and Great Britain, and some observers speculated about war. The British ordered Captain George Vancouver, who had been a midshipman with Cook in 1778, and a small flotilla, to bring the nonsense to an end. Between 1792 and 1794, Vancouver completed comprehensive surveys of British Columbia's most important waterways, including the harbor of the city which now bears his name. After a chance meeting and apparently friendly exchange between Vancouver's ships and those of Galiano and Valdes in June 1792, the Spaniards set sail from English Bay off Point Grey never to return.

Through the first half of the 19th century, Canada's west coast held an irresistible lure for the adventurous: explorers seeking the Northwest Passage, fur traders and foresters who recognized the stately Douglas fir's suitability to mast the great vessels in the Age of Sail. Various pockets of settlement for servicing ships, canning fish and lumbering, sprung up along the coast. Several forts protected the North West Company's fur trade throughout the interior, but it took the Cariboo Gold Rush of 1858 to inject urgency into British efforts to regularize government of the colonies: New Caledonia on the mainland and the separate colony of Vancouver Island, both run by Governor James Douglas from Victoria.

As a typical wilderness colonial headquarters, Victoria was already doing its best to re-create a little piece of England. Douglas, who had arrived earlier to supervise the Hudson's Bay Company's fur trade, and his British cohorts succeeded in establishing at least the pretense of gracious airs. They viewed the happenings on the mainland with disdain, with its riffraff assembly of loggers and mills along Burrard Inlet (eventually Vancouver harbor), and tumultuous riverboat traffic out of the squatters' and prospectors' capital of Queensborough (soon to become New Westminster).

Paddlewheelers and boats of all descriptions navigated the powerful Fraser as far as the canyon's worst rapids. Mercantile commerce created shipping companies that regularly serviced the

Victoria and the colonies developed under the firm hand of Governor James Douglas, who had arrived to supervise the affairs of the Hudson's Bay Company. As his capital attempted to achieve an element of refinement during the 1880s, the sidewheeler S.S. Yosemite is shown in the inner harbor.

entire west coast. As the gold seekers charged to the Cariboo and the more adventurous merchant class from Victoria staked their claim to the mainland's river mouth, British politicians became nervous. The mainland and island colonies were merged into one: British Columbia.

Despite all evidence that the Lower Fraser River Valley—modern Greater Vancouver— would be the economic heart of the colony, Sir James Douglas was firm: the capital would remain in more refined Victoria. His decision dictated that ships and waterways would be the umbilical cord of everyday life in the colony, and, after 1871, in the Province of British Columbia.

This book was published in 1985 to commemorate the 25th anniversary of the provincial government's direct intervention in coastal shipping. During 1958, a series of labor disputes affecting Canadian Pacific Steamships and a relative newcomer, the Black Ball Line, created a sense of helplessness and insecurity to Vancouver Island. When Black Ball employees threatened to strike in sympathy with their CP colleagues, Premier W.A.C. Bennett literally read the riot act. Police arrived at Black Ball terminals to inform officials that the Civil Defense Act had been invoked and that the Black Ball Line was under provincial trusteeship. The employees defied that order and a court injunction. They grudgingly went back to work only after coercive federal legislation was aimed at CP ships. Vancouver Island was spared the possibility of being cut adrift from the mainland.

Bennett then appealed to both Canadian Pacific and Black Ball management, seeking not only assurances that service would be secured but also that fundamental improvements would be made. He complained that the economy of Victoria was in deep decline, for no other reason than total lack of confidence in transportation. Both CP and Black Ball replied that they had no plans to improve service and could offer little solace to Vancouver Island.

With characteristic bravado and determination, W.A.C. Bennett startled the British Columbia public by announcing that the government was going into the ferry business. They would begin with two state-of-the-art ships and a direct link from Victoria to

Vancouver, via Swartz Bay and Tsawwassen respectively. The news was greeted by both mariners and the popular press with much ridicule, cartoons and general merriment. Veteran seamen were particularly convinced that the heavy and unpredictable seas off Tsawwassen Beach made any terminal plans foolhardy in the extreme.

On June 15, 1960, *M.V. Sidney* sailed with the first load of passengers and vehicles to launch what has become one of Canada's greatest shipping success stories. By the end of the decade, BC Ferries became larger than the west coast Royal Canadian Navy, the largest passenger shipping company in Canada, and, by some statistical measurements, the largest ferry fleet in the world. Technical innovations have consistently brought experts from the international shipping community to study various procedures.

When *M.V. Sidney* and *M.V. Tsawwassen* first sailed, the BC Ferry Authority had 191 employees. Over its 25-year history, thousands have served the company. Hundreds are still on the payroll who can boast fifteen or more years' service and many can tell of their previous experience with Black Ball, CP, Gulf Island Ferries or Coast Ferries.

British Columbia Ferry Corporation is one of these, because of these, and all of these.

Development on the British Columbia mainland, spurred on by the Caribou gold rush, was a rough and tumble affair. Queensborough (later New Westminster), served the paddlewheeler traffic (opposite page, 1863-1867) and Burrard Inlet (Vancouver) was a series of sawmills and lumbering operations. (right, circa 1872)

Vancouver Harbor was a thriving concern by the late 1880s (bottom left), leaving little doubt even then that it would be the major urban center of British Columbia. The word "ferry" was becoming part of the language, transporting people, cattle and carriages (top left) through the same decade.

An earlier vessel to serve the coast was Iroquois (right) shown in Pender Harbor Divide in 1910.

The early development of the British Columbia coast was more a matter of exploitation than serious planning: furs, fish, gold and masts for the great sailing ships. Settlers consisted of profiteers and adventurers, few of whom planned to stay for long.

After the explorers, shipping pioneers served the coast from a base at the mouth of the Columbia River at Fort Vancouver, now a Washington State community across from Portland, Oregon. The Hudson's Bay Company vessel, the 101-foot *Beaver,* was to be the most famous of the early traders, traveling the coast as far as the Queen Charlotte Islands for over fifty years. Built in Britain in 1835, she ran aground at Prospect Point, in what is now Vancouver's Stanley Park. Abandoned by her owners, she sat forlornly for four years, decaying in public view until she mercifully washed off the rock and sank in First Narrows.

The Cariboo gold rush of 1858 spawned a brisk riverboat traffic in the Fraser. Many riverboat owners expanded their routes with other vessels serving Victoria and the entire coast as far north as the Stikine River. By the end of the century, the young province had a thriving shipping industry: yards, construction, freight handling facilities and considerable competition.

Another early boat, fondly remembered by historians was *Senator,* which replaced a rowboat ferry across Vancouver Harbor in 1881. The 51-foot vessel charged ten cents for a passenger and fifty cents a head for cattle. She was to end her days as a tugboat.

Two of the earliest companies played a major role in coastal history: The Union Steamship Company and Canadian Pacific Steamships.

The most famous of the early coastal traders, S.S. Beaver, *was to end her days perched ignominiously on the rocks off Vancouver's Stanley Park. She was passed regularly during her final years by the first of the Canadian Pacific's great "white ships,"* Empress of India *(opposite page).*

S.S. Senator *(top) was considered the height of luxury for crossing Vancouver Harbor when she arrived in 1881 and,* S.S. Cutch *(bottom), became the first Union Steamship in British Columbia waters in 1890.*

In 1890, Britain's Union Company, purchased a pleasure craft built for India's Maharaja of Cutch in 1884. After a long journey around Cape Horn, the ship was to launch a seventy-year corporate history close to the hearts of most British Columbians. *Cutch* became the first of dozens of familiar Union Steamship vessels throughout all of the province's waterways.

In 1891, the first of the great Canadian Pacific Railway white ships, *Empress of India,* sailed into Burrard Inlet. But it was not until 1901 that the railway took total control of Canadian Pacific Navigation, previously owned by the Hudson's Bay Company.

The automobile, which changed everything in coastal shipping, was originally ignored. When the first cars appeared, they didn't move very far. Vehicles crossing waterways were handled like freight, most often strapped to the deck of a ship. But human imagination is boundless. Those who insisted upon getting a car to the Gulf Islands usually found a way, even to the point of roping the vehicle on a raft and towing it across. Oldtimers on Salt Spring Island remember an ingenious chap from Victoria who launched the first Swartz Bay to Fulford Harbor ferry. He mounted two old Buicks on the back of a big scow, jacked up the rear end, ran heavy belts to the vessel's propeller, and let the cars drive the ferry. He could transport four vehicles at a time for paying customers.

Canadian Pacific carried cars grudgingly, but eventually responded to the rapidly growing market. Most larger company vessels were adapted to carry some vehicles but even the famed sisters, *Princess Kathleen* and the first *Princess Marguerite,* delivered in 1925, could only accommodate about thirty. All key ships rigidly clung to the standard "alongside" berthing facilities in Vancouver, Nanaimo and Victoria, with cars loading and unloading though side doors onto passenger and cargo piers.

LOVER OF THE UNIVERSE

Talented eccentrics have played dominant roles throughout British Columbia's colorful history. Few are more noted in the early years than William Alexander Smith, a native of Nova Scotia. Attracted to California by the lure of gold, he sought and received from the State Legislature a special act changing his name to Amor De Cosmos, which he defined as "Lover of the Universe."

After news that gold had been found farther north at Barkerville in 1858, De Cosmos made his way to Victoria, where he established a year later, not a gold mine, but a newspaper, *The Weekly British Colonist.* The name changed ultimately to "Daily" and finally, became *The Colonist.* As a newspaper editor and, subsequently, as an elected politician, De Cosmos soon became Governor James Douglas' greatest source of aggravation. He led successful campaigns for responsible government and for the merger of the two British Columbia colonies. When the province became a part of Canada, De Cosmos held seats in both the provincial legislature and the federal parliament in Ottawa. From 1872 - 1874, he also served as Premier of British Columbia, resigning the post only after federal law forbade the dual roles. He remained a federal Member of Parliament until 1882.

Amor De Cosmos was a man of remarkable foresight. When Vancouver Island transportation links were debated during the 1880's, he first supported a grand scheme of railway bridges, beginning at Bute Inlet and including a massive span over Seymour Narrows. He angered the railways, however, in 1889 by favoring a different method. He thought a rail ferry would be the only sensible route. De Cosmos studied the long finger of the Saanich Peninsula extending from Victoria Harbor toward the mainland, finally concluding that Swartz Bay at the peninsula's tip should be the ferry terminus. His proposal was for a Victoria, Saanich and New Westminster railway, crossing the water by ferry at 20 knots in one hour and ten minutes. Although in 1903 various rail companies tried to resurrect a similar proposal, nothing was to come of the idea for about seventy years.

Amor De Cosmos was among the first to foresee that the best route between Victoria and the mainland, would use the mouth of the Fraser River. David Thorne's drawing shows the ship Victorian, *at Port Guichon, in 1903.*

THE BLACK BALL LINE

The Canadian Pacific was still having things its own way in the trunk routes between the mainland and Vancouver Island by 1950. The various *Princesses,* awkward with automobiles, plied from Vancouver Harbor to both Nanaimo and Victoria. The 6.5-hour liesurely sail from Victoria at midnight was frequently the only service the capital received, and sleeping accommodations would regularly sell out.

But tough competition arrived from the south in 1951 in the personage of Captain Alexander Marshall Peabody and his Black Ball Line, a company dating back to the 19th century and the age of sail. Peabody himself apprenticed in a company four-masted barque at the age of 15. His family's Puget Sound Navigation Company had played a key role in the earliest development of British Columbia shipping.

In 1948, the State of Washington decided to go into the ferry business, buying much of the Puget Sound fleet, but Peabody kept a few vessels to himself, tying them up until he could plot his next move. He studied the appallingly poor service in British Columbia and sensed a profitable opportunity.

Peabody arrived on the scene with the venerable *Kahloke,* and followed up by adding four more vessels: *Bainbridge, Quillayute,* the sparkling *Chinook* and an old steamship, *Smokwa.* Black Ball built terminals at Horseshoe Bay on the mainland and at Departure Bay outside Nanaimo, also pioneering service to the Sunshine Coast and in Jervis Inlet. Despite engineering problems with some of the vessels, the service was quick, efficient and generally put CP to shame. The railway began to take a beating.

37

The coastal service of the Canadian Pacific was the dominant theme of seafaring development for the first half of the 20th century. The many vessels would wedge tightly into Victoria's Inner Harbor (left), sometimes three and four abreast.

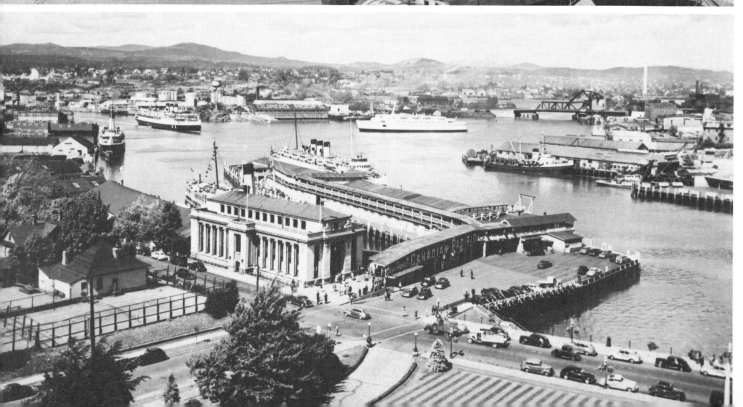

CP pioneered service to the Gulf Islands as well. M.V. Motor Princess, when she arrived in 1923, carried 40 cars. Renamed Pender Queen, *her final 20 years of work were within the BC Ferries fleet.*

THE GULF ISLANDS

The first large ferry boat specifically designed to carry cars to arrive on the coast was *Daily,* built at Tacoma, Washington in 1913. She could carry up to 18 cars and over 100 people. CP purchased her in 1918 and she emerged from refit with a new name: *Island Princess.* The larger *Motor Princess,* built at Esquimalt, appeared in 1923. The two wooden hull vessels were to have a long and happy life in British Columbia.

Victoria newspaper publisher Sam Matson, annoyed by irregular service to the Gulf Islands, purchased *Island Princess* from CP in 1930, establishing the Gulf Islands Ferry Company. The vessel went in for refit and she emerged with a new name honoring a British Columbia war hero, Colonel Cyrus W. Peck, VC, DSO. Matson hired Captain George A. Maude to run the new operation and *Cy Peck* became a beloved mainstay of islands service until 1966.

The Gulf Islands Ferry Company was taken over by a group of investors in 1951 headed by prominent Salt Spring businessman Gavin Mouat. The new owners convinced W.A.C. Bennett to give them a subsidy in 1955. They purchased *Motor Princess* from CP, and brought another vessel from the State of Washington. She would become *M.V. George S. Pearson.*

As service to the islands was beginning to take shape, another coastal legend was into the ferry busness as well. Oswald H. "Sparky" New started a log towing concern in 1937 and gradually evolved into various aspects of coastal freight services. In 1946 he began Coast Ferries with the vessel *Brentwood* running between the Saanich Peninsula and the Malahat, replacing her with the 16-car *M.V. Mill Bay* in 1956. Sparky New commissioned a new boat in 1958: the second *Island Princess,* sporting not only a 20-car capacity, but also four double staterooms.

Sparky New's two vessels Mill Bay *and* Island Princess *did not join B.C. Ferries until 1969. The latter was significantly enlarged by BC Ferries, and now sails as* North Island Princess.

Captain George Maude began his Gulf Islands ferry service in 1930, acquiring the then 17-year-old Daily *from Washington State. Renamed* Cy Peck *(top), she was to be finally retired by BC Ferries in 1966. The interior of M.V.* Motor Princess *(bottom) was considered to be state-of-the-art in her day.*

The flags and bunting were in abundance in 1930 when Cy Peck *started service between Salt Spring Island's Fulford Harbor and Swartz Bay on Vancouver Island (bottom left and right). A later Gulf Islands ferry, also acquired from the State of Washington, M.V. George S. Pearson (top), was retired by BC Ferries in 1966.*

W.A.C. BENNETT

Captain Alex Peabody arrived in British Columbia just as a new government was forming. Seizing upon the failure of both the Liberal and Conservative parties to win a clear legislature majority, a maverick MLA from Kelowna, Cecil Bennett, had forged a new alliance under the banner of Social Credit, assuming power in 1952. Nothing in the province would ever be the same again, particularly the lives of those who dared get in the way of British Columbia public policy. Survival-of-the-fittest pioneer west coast history was truly over.

When he was certain of his oft-discussed "vision," and of its subsequent effects, William Andrew Cecil Bennett brought new meaning to the word "stubborn." He was unmovable, and the carcasses of those who begged to differ litter three decades of British Columbia history. He was a master of delegation and flexible in private, but his grander view of provincial development was non-negotiable. His emotion was equally profound and his tears would occasionally appear at political rallies.

"The opposition never learned how to handle me, they always criticized—I loved that," Bennett told an interviewer long after he left office. "That just got my blood going. But if they praised me. . . well I would have cried."

The architect of modern British Columbia was born September 6, 1900, in a small village near Fundy National Park, New Brunswick, but in 1901, the family moved to Hampton, N.B. As a young teenager in Hampton and later in nearby Saint John, Bennett developed an early love of politics, attending every meeting possible, listening to many of the era's best orators.

While working for a Saint John hardware store in 1918, Bennett joined the air force, but he failed in repeated attempts to get overseas before the first world war ended. At one point he became so frustrated with the Saint John recruiting office that he paid his own way by train to Camp Borden, Ontario where he demanded action. The air force calmly shipped him back home. He was told to be patient. But adventure was in Bennett's blood, and in 1919, he decided to travel west.

After eleven years working for the Marshall Wells hardware organization in Edmonton, a period that included his marriage to May Richards, he settled in British Columbia's Okanagan Valley. There he began to build his family, his own hardware organization, the friendships that would last a lifetime, and a passionate love affair with British Columbia.

Conservative politics was never far from his heart. Following an unsuccessful federal attempt, he was elected to the British Columbia Legislature in 1941, stepping down in 1947 to lose yet again on the federal front. Back in the provincial house to stay after a 1948 by-election, W.A.C. Bennett was soon to find himself at the vortex of political change. At first, he was rebuffed in an attempt to wrest control of the provincial Progressive Conservative Party from leaders dominated by the Liberals in a coalition government.

He then looked toward neighboring Alberta, and the Social Credit government of Ernest C. Manning. The movement had some support in British Columbia. By 1951, the high profile name of W.A.C. Bennett won the leadership of the Social Credit League of British Columbia. In 1952, the Bennett-led Progressive Conservative refugees and the rump group of committed didactic social creditors, became the government. For the rest of his life he would deny that Social Credit had been merely his instrument of convenience to obtain power.

The written philosophies of Major C.H. Douglas literally meant "social credit," the presumption that the credit of the collective public would always be able to pay off debts accrued during recessionary times. When money was in short supply, Douglas advocated printing as much money as necessary to meet the demand. Economists quickly debunked the theory as "funny money," and disastrously inflationary. However, the philosophy took political root in various parts of the English-speaking world, especially in Canada's Province of Alberta. For decades, William Aberhart and his successor, Ernest Manning, ruled Alberta under the banner of Social Credit. W.A.C. Bennett's political philosophy was unique and

Captain Alex Peabody and his Black Ball Line would dramatically change the style of ferry transport in British Columbia. The vessels and terminals were designed for no-nonsense drive-on, drive-off service and, through most of the 1950s, the efficiency put the Canadian Pacific to shame. Shown to the left are Kahloke, *originally built in 1903, and Quillayute.*

independent. Questioned as to whether he was an adherent to Major Douglas' theories, he would merely mutter, "nothing wrong with it," and then quickly change the topic of conversation. To this day, however, some visitors to British Columbia fail to understand that the name "Social Credit" is merely a home-grown label, and that Victoria's Douglas Street is in honor of the first governor, Sir James Douglas.

During the first years of his government, ferry service was low on the priority list. Bennett did what he could to help entrepreneurs like Gavin Mouat and Sparky New build their small systems throughout the islands, but he was less than pleased to be dependent upon the vagaries of the Canadian Pacific Railway and the American-owned Black Ball for the very livelihood of Vancouver Island. Nanaimo enjoyed its new-found Black Ball service through the 1950s, but Victoria was in desperate shape. The premier watched and waited.

It took a series of labor problems to generate reaction, but when W.A.C. Bennett decided to move, it was with high drama and determination.

S.S. Smokwa was the last steam powered ferry on the North American west coast, she and Bainbridge were to cause B.C. Ferries mechanical nightmares. Ladies frequently complained that when they walked over the wooden decks of Bainbridge, their high heels would poke right through the floorboards.

The most modern of the Black Ball ships was M.V. Chinook II, built in Seattle in 1947. Here she is shown being repainted in the pastel blue of The Dogwood Fleet. She served B.C. Ferries as Sechelt Queen until 1976, when she was tranferred to the Ministry of Highways for service between Powell River and Comox.

Ferry line-ups, and various individual approaches to killing the time, have frequently been a part of modern British Columbia life. Here a 1960 photo shows Horseshoe Bay. M.V. Bainbridge, at her dock, could carry a maximum of 45 cars. The current generation of BC Ferries ships carry between 360 and 400 vehicles. It is rare that anyone is left behind.

CHAOS AND INTERVENTION
CHAPTER THREE

"This disaster can be ranked with a drought or crop failure in its effect on our people, and the result to those people dependent on this tourist industry is economic hardship and misery."—The Associated Chambers of Commerce of Vancouver Island, in a 1958 letter to Prime Minister John Diefenbaker.

In most parts of the world, when the word "disaster" is used, it is a reference to war, carnage, floods, hurricanes, mine cave-ins and assorted other calamities. Throughout the islands of British Columbia, the word applies to ferry shutdowns, whether real or threatened: The paranoia grew from a history of irregular, unpredictable and poor quality service. A severing of the lines of communication is not only a danger to avoid, but also catastrophic. The *unthinkable* happened in 1958.

It is inconceivable that inadequate ferry service between the mainland and Vancouver Island could have been tolerated in perpetuity. The private sector's need to curry favor with the traveling public, the forces of competition, and the politician's passion for popularity would doubtlessly have brought about significant improvement over what existed in 1958, with or without government intervention.

THE LABOR CRISIS

Canadian Pacific Steamships and the Black Ball Line were dealing with three unions by the late 1950s: the Canadian Merchant Service Guild, the National Association of Marine Engineers and the Seafarers' International Union. Most of the contracts governing the emloyees of the two systems expired toward the end of 1957, but negotiations carried on well into 1958. By April, CP crews were demanding 25 percent increases (Black Ball unions were content to wait and seek a matching settlement) but the best a conciliation board would offer was 10 percent.

The two shipping companies operated under different labor laws. Canadian Pacific, a subsidiary of the federally chartered railway,

The controversy led to a new shipping company, and a ridiculed terminal location at Tsawwassen was to become the most sophisticated ferry base in the world.

dealt with Ottawa. Black Ball unions fell under British Columbia statutes. In longshore and seafaring matters, arrangements made at the senior national level would soon become the benchmark for local agreements.

On May 17, 1958, the SIU walked out on Canadian Pacific, a strike that lasted until July 26. Days later, the Black Ball unions gave their executives a strike mandate and it was publicly threatened. Marine Engineers and the Guild issued a 72-hour strike warning to Black Ball management. Meanwhile, a federal mediator was trying to work out a CP agreement.

W.A.C. Bennett met with the three unions on June 17. He said in an interview years later that the Black Ball union representatives told him that they would be happy to work for the government, but not their employer. At the conclusion of the meeting, Bennett announced that the Civil Defence Act had been invoked and that Black Ball was under trusteeship. Police read the riot act at the terminals the next day.

As federal mediators continued to sort out the CP Steamships strike, Bennett began meetings with business leaders, including Captain Alexander Peabody of Black Ball and CP officials. All consulted business executives told Premier Bennett that greatly improved ferry services, particularly a direct connection between the mainland and Victoria, would be neither practical nor profitable. They offered little optimism for labor stability or dependable service, convincing the premier that they wanted the government to solve their labor crisis. Bennett offered to subsidize the development of highways and terminals to stimulate better services, but the corporate executives retreated into a vague shell, waiting for a better offer. The government offered to spend one million dollars on highways and terminals for Peabody's Jervis Inlet and Powell River service.

Sitting quietly in the background was a Bennett friend who became the single most important outside motivator in the establishment of a government ferry service—Captain Harry Terry, President of Northland Navigation Ltd. It would be years before the enormity of Terry's involvement was clearly understood.

Exasperated by the pessimism of business people, Bennett considered his options. When he asked Cap' Terry if a government

service from Victoria to the mainland was feasible, Terry was encouraging. He provided the premier with a solid professional understanding. Bennett had his ace card in hand. It was suggested by some observers that Bennett's strategy from the outset was to take over the ferries. Both Phil Gaglardi and Monty Aldous, instrumental in the ferry development, said in 1985 that the decision was made by the premier only after every other possibility had failed.

However, a total lack of progress on the labor front finally forced Premier Bennett's hand. The Canadian Merchant Service Guild and the National Association of Marine Engineers engaged in a strike with Black Ball on July 18. The islands of British Columbia were cut adrift.

From Victoria, Premier Bennett announced not only that the government was going to take the unions to court for defying the Civil Defence Act, he stunned the province with the announcement that the government was going to provide a proper ferry service. BC Ferries were born in theory, if not in practice, on July 18, 1958.

Following the announcement, matters tumbled into place quickly. Black Ball employees, after first ignoring a court injunction, were back to work on July 24 and the determined provincial action on the west coast prodded federal authorities to wrap up the Canadian Pacific dispute. Federal legislation forced CP crews back to the ships on July 26. There would be a few brief wildcat strikes, but with a 22 percent wage hike, all the union contracts were finally signed on January 30, 1959.

An island was built in the saltchuk, a mile out from Tsawwassen Beach, and the causeway worked back toward shore (opposite page). Isolation made the terminal expandable.

THE BUILDER

The British Columbia entry into the ferry industry was unfolded in lightning fashion. Bennett turned it over to his highways minister, Phillip A. Gaglardi. The minister was told that nothing but the best would do.

Gaglardi, the irrepressible hustings-stomping evangelical orator from Kamloops, as he raced through the province, would leave controversy in his wake like clouds of dust rising from a Euclid truck in a construction zone. But he got things done, frequently thumbing his nose at bureaucratic procedures and even legislative budget controls. After annual construction contracts were completed each fall, and if the snows held off, Gaglardi would order construction crews to keep going. He knew that the sooner the work got done—this year rather than next—the cheaper it would be. He worried about paying the bills and budgetary approval later. As his contractor friends grew wealthy, nasty rumors began to circulate alleging various financial misdeeds. Not one charge was ever proven, save the obvious: the contract awarded by sealed tender was frequently and dramatically changed by Gaglardi's months of roadside improvisations.

Through it all, even his severest critics were forced to concede that no one could build highways like the Rev. P.A. Gaglardi. He simply wouldn't accept the word "impossible," be it conquering a treacherous mountain pass, dumping hundreds of thousands of tons of sawdust as the foundation for the Trans-Canada Highway through the marshlands of Burnaby, or taming the mouth of the Fraser River.

W.A.C. Bennett described his bold ventures and passionate belief in British Columbia, as "vision." He and his wife were rarely more content than when they relaxed on Salt Spring Island. To this day, May Bennett, mother of the current premier, treasures her lieftime BC Ferries "gold pass."

Only a friend would have been able to capture this mood. The photograph was taken by "Big Jim" Ryan of Victoria.

One of the originals, Queen of Tsawwassen (bottom), greets a sister in Active Pass.

The Deas Tunnel, on the freeway to the State of Washington, was a spectacular engineering feat. Many engineers warned that the combined dangers of tidal action, the shifting sandy base and the fear of strong spring freshets could combine to wash a $35 million project into the sea. He once described the Deas Tunnel as "a triumph of vision and imagination over hard engineering reality."

Gaglardi was still taking bows for that achievement when the boss, W.A.C. Bennett, announced in 1958 that British Columbia was going into the ferry business. The highways minister was put in charge of constructing the ships and terminals. Armed with a budget of $9 million (it would ultimately cost $12 million), full powers of expropriation, and all the cabinet support he needed, Gaglardi pressed on.

THE SHIPS

Determining the ship design was the first priority. British Columbia began its shipping enterprise with such speed and political determination, there was insufficient time to shop for naval architecture. Coincidentally, a vessel was under construction for Bob Acheson's Black Ball Transport (independent of the Black Ball Line) to service Port Angeles, Victoria, Puget Sound and Seattle. *M.V. Coho* seemed perfect for British Columbia's purposes, with minor blueprint alterations to permit bow and stern loading. Her designer, Seattle naval architect Phillip F. Spaulding, was retained with only one stipulation: he must find a British Columbia partner. He and Arthur McLaren opened a Vancouver office and went to work.

"It was a bold stroke on the part of Gaglardi to move ahead without all the background together," Spaulding recalls. "Right there is the significance of the BC Ferry system. . .the decision-making that man did right on the spot."

After approving ship design, tenders were called. Victoria Machinery Depot won the first and Burrard Drydock of North Vancouver got the contract for the second. Keels were laid for the two ships on May 9, 1959. *M.V. Sidney* was in the water by October 6 and *M.V. Tsawwassen* rolled down the slip on November 28. Final fitting out and sea trials would take many more months.

Gaglardi took a personal hand in almost every detail. At one point he flew to England to choose the engines for the first two ships, opting for 16-cylinder Mirrlees Twins. As BC Ferries grew, lower public tenders awarded engine contracts for the next four ships to other manufacturers. They all proved totally unsatisfactory. The Mirrlees were back to stay in 1964 and those still in the fleet are performing well in 1985.

THE TERMINALS

From a press and political point of view, the selection, design and construction of the ships were minor asides, but the choice of mainland and Victoria terminals was testy and controversial. Once again Phil Gaglardi was to face the scorn of engineering experts. When Tsawwassen Beach, an area once known as English Bluff, was being investigated as the mainland terminal, critics howled that it was madness. They warned of weather and the frequently rough waters. Every inch of coast was explored from Steveston to White Rock, but always the finger on the map came back to a spot near the Indian reserve of Tsawwassen.

The minister conducted his own survey, polling twenty sea captains who knew the waters well. "Ten of them said yes, and ten of them said no," Gaglardi recalled. "So we decided to go ahead. I figured the positives cancelled out the negatives and the negatives substantiated the positives." Illogical as that may sound, Gaglardi has always protested that he never operated by whim. He said he surrounded himself with the brightest young engineering minds he could find. "The ideas were not mine, I just made them happen," Gaglardi said. His Tsawwassen confidence was endorsed when the respected engineering firm, Swan Wooster, finally took the contract.

There was less ridicule but no less debate over the Victoria terminus. All eyes first focused on the town of Sidney, where the established berth served vessels heading to the American San Juan Islands and Washington State. But experts warned repeatedly that the waters off Sidney were insufficiently sheltered, and that the added

distance from the mainland would make a two-hour shuttle schedule almost impossible. Beyond Sidney and the end of blacktop, a bumpy dirt road led to the tip of the Saanich Peninsula, and Gavin Mouat's funky little Gulf Islands ferry dock. The location, unheard of by many at the time, was Swartz Bay—perfect from every point of view. The difference between Sidney and Swartz Bay, in fuel savings alone, was calculated to be $80,000 annually. The choices of Tsawwassen and Swartz Bay fullfilled the seventy-year-old prophecy of Amor De Cosmos.

Bulldozers plowed an extension of the Patricia Bay Highway toward Swartz Bay where a terminal soon began construction. An artificial island was placed a mile from shore in the saltchuck at Tsawwassen. A new seven-mile highway was built from the Deas Tunnel to the beach, as a one-mile causeway worked from the sea toward land.

Phil Gaglardi remembers with considerable amusement the formidable barrage of press condemnation and ridicule during the development of the ships and terminals. "One guy called it the stupidest plan that could ever be brought in. Others said I was the one who was going to break the government. I was called 'Commodore Gaglardi' and the ferries were known as 'Gaglardi's navy'. The cartoonists loved it," he said. By the time the first vessel was ready for acceptance from the builder, Gaglardi said even his cabinet colleagues had come to believe the press. He had arranged for a major party at Victoria Machinery Depot and invited the entire cabinet to join the dignitaries. "I couldn't get any cabinet ministers to come—it was considered to be a complete flop." Gaglardi managed to badger colleagues Lyle Wicks and Les Peterson to attend the ceremony, but even W.A.C. Bennett found something else to do that day.

The mood started to change once the ship left drydock and began her final fitting out and sea trials. By the time the service was inaugurated, media coverage had improved considerably and W.A.C. Bennett's faith was restored. At that point, BC Ferries became his baby, and his colorful Minister of Highways was gradually phased out of the picture.

ONLY THE BEGINNING

For Seattle naval architect Phil Spaulding and his Vancouver partner Art McLaren, the first two vessels for the BC Ferries were just the opening salvo. For Spaulding, who has designed tankers, freighters, gunboats for a global clientele (he is currently developing a huge theatrical paddle wheeler for the Grand Ole Opry), and many of the prominent vessels for the States of Alaska and Washington, BC Ferries retains a special status.

After the first two ships became a substantial success, BC Ferries original general manager, Monty Aldous, was soon back in Seattle to have Spaulding design two more, with expansion and modifications based on experience. In these discussions, British Columbia offered to buy out the plans, avoiding future royalties.

Spaulding is amused to this day by his lack of business foresight at the time. "They had two ships and were building two more. How many could they possibly want? I sold the plans for something like $25,000." Aldous insists that the one-shot payment was $10,000. When *Queen of Burnaby* entered the fleet in 1964, she became the ninth Spaulding capital ship of the BC Ferries.

The naval architect's happy relations with British Columbia were redeemed almost a decade later, when his successful Washington State Ferries double-enders *Spokane* and *Walla Walla* became the inspiration for British Columbia's "super-ferries." Spaulding designed the five *Cowichan-Class* vessels, the largest double-ended ships in the world.

Yet the architect plays down his own role. "The real story is what they have done with the ships—stretching, lifting, re-engining, and constantly adapting the design. . .really quite awesome."

Phil Gaglardi (left), enjoying a ferry sailing with Captain Harry Terry.

THE CAPTAIN

When W.A.C. Bennett needed expert guidance and encouragement in the face of ferry difficulties, he turned to a friend who had been a coastal shipping legend for decades, Captain Harold John Cameron Terry. Behind the scenes as the decisions were made, the anonymous role of Harry Terry was the greatest single non-government input in the establishment of BC Ferries.

Terry had gone to sea on a six-masted barque in his native Australia at the age of fourteen, landing a few years later on the British Columbia coast. As a coastal seaman, master, marine superintendant, ship owner and proprietor of a succession of companies evolving into Northland Navigation Ltd., Cap' Terry was a household name in every seaside community from Washington to Alaska. His best ships Canadian Prince (originally CP's Princess Norah) and Northland Prince were not only cargo workhorses, they also offered fine dining saloons and accommodation.

The Captain told Bennett how his difficulties could be solved.

FLYING PHIL

Phil Gaglardi raised eyebrows with his propensity for speeding tickets as he raced though the province building highways. "I was testing the curves," he frequently protested. "I built 'em. Someone had to test 'em." But it was an aircraft that was to earn Flying Phil his nickname and his severest political difficulties.

The gentlemanly pace of W.A.C. Bennett's government—traveling by road, train and ship wherever possible—was altogether too slow for Gaglardi. His style was "hands on," simultaneously running bridge and highways contracts throughout the vastness of British Columbia, while also managing a department in Victoria. He would often annoy the premier by missing cabinet meetings.

A pilot friend proposed the ideal solution—a private plane. The highways minister immediately went to bounce the general idea off the premier. Bennett asked Gaglardi to get him a report. The pilot returned days later to advise that a chap in the southern U.S. named Bill Lear seemed to have the ideal aircraft at a rental of a mere $5,000 per month. Gaglardi was convinced that Bennett's answer would be negative. He would have to plot his strategy carefully. He wouldn't have long to wait.

Premier Bennett soon after invited his highways minister to join him on a trip to Prince Rupert. This was the opportunity, but Gaglardi was coy, "I don't know, Cec. The long drive to Kelsey Bay, the ship to Rupert. . .the speeches and return. It could be three or four days," Gaglardi said. "I'll get back to you."

The solution was a small float plane. Gaglardi and his pilot circled over Prince Rupert as Queen of Prince Rupert, carrying the premier, approached her berth. The plane swooped in and Gaglardi jumped aboard ship to greet his boss. In speech after speech that day, Phil Gaglardi sang the praises of W.A.C. Bennett. "By the time we were back on the ship, Cec was high as a kite. We were hanging over the rail, looking down at my little seaplane," Gaglardi recounts.

The minister reminded Bennett of the previous chat about the need for an airplane. The premier conceded that it was probably a good idea. Gaglardi said he just happened to have a contract with him for approval. With one more glance at the float plane, Bennett signed the document and the Lear Jet was soon on its way to British Columbia.

"I used to trick him quite a bit," Gaglardi remembers with a mischievious grin. Asked if there were reprecussions when the jet arrived, Flying Phil replied, "Do you think that W.A.C. Bennett would ever admit—even to me—that he signed a document without reading it?"

SOCIALISM IF NECESSARY

"We are a young country; we must build on the solid rock of sound economic policies and balanced budgets. But we must be prepared, as a nation, to step from the solid rock onto new ground. The path of ease, the path of tradition alone, is not the path of a greater Canada."— W.A.C. Bennett, addressing the Canadian Chamber of Commerce in 1962.

Few Canadian politicians have made as much fuss about socialism as W.A.C. Bennett. In blustery election verbiage, he would warn that "the red hordes are at the gate." Yet political economists could argue that he had a keen understanding of where public intervention in the marketplace was the only sensible avenue to be pursued. He refused to allow that chaos was ever desirable or acceptable, even that created by unbridled free enterprise.

"Socialism if necessary, but not necessarily socialism," he was fond of saying. He said his style was to attack serious issues "not with a dream in mind, but with hardware in hand."

After Premier Bennett's bold move into the ferry business and, particularly, after the takeover of the BC Electric Company in 1961, he was attacked with rhetoric by business leaders across the country, even using the word communist.

He responded in 1962 by telling business leaders he had inherited a bankrupt, ridiculed PGE railway in 1952. The Pacific Great Eastern, known in the press as "Prince George Eventually," and "Please Go Easy," started nowhere and went nowhere. Bennett said, "I couldn't give it away so we decided to build it and to run it." He said he appealed to the private sector to operate a dependable ferry service, but businessmen said it couldn't be profitable. Hydro, the Columbia River Treaty and the Peace River development could only proceed under government guarantee.

Phil Spaulding is shown aboard M.V. Columbia, *which he designed for Alaska State Ferries. Washington State's* Hyak, *designed by his partner George Nickum, is in the background,*

THE ARCHITECT

British Columbia moved with such extraordinary haste in the development of ferries, there was little time to design ships from scratch. Renowned Seattle naval architect, Phillip Field Spaulding, was retained. He fondly remembers his first days working for the inimitable P.A. Gaglardi.

Phil Spaulding still chuckles at the memory of the acceptance of the first ship, M.V. Sidney, *as she began her sea trials. "It was a cold, miserable day. It had snowed the night before." But the Reverend Gaglardi arrived with full confidence that Divine Providence would perform on schedule.*

"I'll never forget that day. The sun broke through. It was beautiful, and Gaglardi thanked God for his co-operation," Spaulding said.

The choice of Swartz Bay as the Victoria terminus in 1960, followed a less bitter debate than that which had focused on Tsawwassen, but there were many who thought the established dock at Sidney should have been utilized. The "mudhole" of Swartz Bay (top) under construction in 1960, and how it evolved (below).

The Black Ball Line turned
the sedate fishing village of
Horseshoe Bay into a major
ferry terminal, but it was BC
Ferries that started the heavy
construction (top) to make the
congested quarters suitable
for heavy volume traffic.
Horseshoe Bay in the modern
era (below).

Departure Bay, Nanaimo.

The fourth day of the heavy volume terminals, along with Tsawwassen, Swartz Bay and Horseshoe Bay, is Nanaimo's Departure Bay (extreme left), pioneered in the 1950s by Captain Alex Peabody and the Black Ball Line. But smaller facilities throughout the system are equally important to the local populations.

(From left to right, top row) - Vesuvious (Salt Spring Island), Crofton (south of Nanaimo), Saturna Island, Brentwood Bay (Saanich Peninsula) and Saltery Bay (near Powell River).

(Centre row) - Sturdies Bay (Galiano Island), Langdale, Earl's Cove (Jervis Inlet), Snug Cove (Bowen Island), and Mill Bay (base of the Malahat).

(Bottom row) - Montague (Galiano), Village Bay (Mayne Island), Long Harbor (Salt Spring Island), Otter Bay (North Pender Island) and Fulford Harbor (Salt Spring Island).

"He (W.A.C. Bennett) gave me one instruction: he wanted the best ferry service in the world."—M.F. Aldous, General Manager, BC Ferries (1960-1974)

When *M.V. Sidney* and *M.V. Tsawwassen* first sailed on June 15, 1960, not even a psychic would have dared to predict the excitement, success and expansion that was to follow. By 1966, a twenty-four-ship fleet was in place featuring ten major and four minor vessels built in British Columbia, and ten more ships absorbed from other systems.

"If we knew what we were doing it wouldn't have happened," said several key people from the early days. They refused to accept conventional wisdom about anything, forging ahead on their wits and hard work. The terminal agent at Swartz Bay, Denny Keen, frequently slept overnight in his office. Catering superintendent Bill Lowe came to Keen after the two ships had operated for a month. He brought a large box full of cash register receipts from the cafeterias asking what was to be done with them. "We never did figure them out," Keen remembers. Frank Ramsay, a Black Ball veteran who is currently assistant general manager, operations, says his daughter Juanita, born June 30, 1960, was the youngest "employee" of the company. On his babysitting days, the little girl would make the Swartz Bay vault her daytime home, catered to by the women of the staff. Keen recalls, "I used to go visit her in the vault."

It was pandemonium. Staff members were so excited by it all that they'd come down on their days off to see how everything was going, frequently pitching in to solve problems. Many took their families on ferry trips as a happy outing.

M.V. Sidney & M.V. Tsawwassen *were instant success stories, except for an unpredicted demand upon dining facilities. The problem was solved within the first few months. As the ships (left) were constructed and the solution (right).*

THE COMPANY

The ships and terminals were well under construction before the government gave any thought to how the system should be operated. Once again, Captain Harry Terry played a crucial role. The temptation was to simply place the system under the highways ministry, which had been operating a large fleet of small vessels thoughout the province for years. Terry convinced Premier Bennett that what he was developing had the potential to be a major Canadian shipping company. It deserved to stand alone.

The principle of autonomy was etched into political stone from day one, but as a matter of financial convenience, the ferries were placed under the umbrella of another provincial cash flow agency, The British Columbia Toll Bridges Authority. Its name was soon changed to Ferry and Toll Bridges Authority. As the tolls came off the last bridge during the 1960s, the agency became simply the BC Ferry Authority.

After the decision to set up an independent management structure for BC Ferries, the government passed an order-in-council on January 2, 1960, appointing three people to put the company together—General Manager Monty Aldous, Assistant General Manager Ron Worley and Marine Superintendant William B. Weston.

The reasons for Ron Worley's appointment were never fully explained to anyone by W.A.C. Bennett. A political aide and friend, Worley's assignment was likely just to be a political liason for and a watchdog over the government newcomers who were to put the system together. As Worley attempted to define the limits of his own power, he would cause as much consternation as assistance.

Ship construction was frenetic through the early years of BC Ferries. Queen of Saanich, *hitting the water, and* Queen of Esquimalt, *are shown at Victoria Machinery Depot (left), and* City of Vancouver, *bottom right, is shown ready for launching at North Vancouver's Burrard drydock. Clockwise from the top, right, are: VMD president Harold Husband, a principal BC Ferries builder; an ever-popular early cafeteria, and one of the first* M.V. Sidney *crews.*

Worley's most significant contribution came in the area of marketing and promotion, convincing the public to "follow the birds to Victoria," and to have confidence in government ferries. His British Columbia promotional efforts in California were so successful that he earned the nickname, "Hollywood Ron." Despite those achievements, during the seven years he was aboard, Worley's self-defined political role was often viewed as meddlesome.

Bill Weston, to the contrary, was the engineering wizard who built the hardware of the fleet. A native of northern England, he first trained as an auto mechanic, serving as an engineer in the Royal Army. Following military service, he acquired ship engineering expertise and worked for several companies in Canada. He came to BC Ferries after long service in the Canadian north with the ships of the Yukon & White Pass Railway.

Monty Aldous was born near the Indian reserve of Metlakatla, not far from Prince Rupert, on November 21, 1915. His mother, the daughter of a northern pioneer, raised him while his father was off to war. The family reunited in Vancouver after the war and Aldous was educated in the city's public school system. His career unfolded through a series of jobs up and down the British Columbia coast in logging camps and canneries. He was timekeeper, store manager and, for a while, an oil company salesman. For almost two decades prior to his BC Ferries appointment, Aldous held various managerial positions within North Vancouver-based warehouse, fish packing and shipping organizations.

Recalling his first meeting with Premier Bennett, Aldous said Captain Peabody of Black Ball argued that BC Ferries should lop off the bows of their ships to increase the ease of berthing and loading. "He was determined to make our ships look as ugly as his." Bennett decided firmly against the proposal.

Few items thrilled W.A.C. Bennett more than BC Ferries events. Here he hams it up with Gavin Mouat, from whom he acquired Gulf Islands Navigation Company.

"Right then I knew the Chief was going to be a guy I'd like to work with—there was no hesitation about anything," Aldous said. The new general manager emerged from that first meeting with another interesting memory. Peabody, describing Cap' Terry, said, "You know that guy didn't talk very much about himself—he's a Canadian, not an American."

The three order-in-council appointees, Aldous, Worley and Weston, were dispatched to build their company.

The "Susy Q." — Sunshine Coast Queen.

THE ASSIGNMENT

The first major task was to create public confidence in the face of considerable skepticism. Many in high profile positions appeared to be not only critical of the venture, but hoping for a political fiasco. Aldous told anyone who would listen, "If we can get by this first year without a major incident of any kind, then we will be on the road. We will have the confidence of the traveling public." As a precaution against problems, he insisted upon reserve docks on both sides, a $100,000 inventory of spare parts and a company philosophy of courtesy, public service and punctuality. These attributes, he believed, were no longer applicable to Canadian Pacific ships.

The government had received several negative reports about the prospects of the new undertaking. "Any time all the experts say something is doomed to failure, I figure it's bound to be a success as long as you apply yourself," Aldous said. Captain Peabody predicted that BC Ferries would not be able to divert more than 5 percent of the Vancouver-Victoria traffic carried by the airlines in 1960. One year later, BC Ferries had taken 95 percent of the business. Air Canada, which had offered twenty-two flights a day between the two cities prior to the ferries, cut back to six flights by 1962.

Aldous achieved the incident-free first year and the resulting public confidence for which he had prayed. "The good Lord blessed us, because by golly it was just unreal."

Through the 1960s, the construction of ships, the absorption of other coastal companies and the expansion of routes, terminals and service continued non-stop until the fleet had reached 24 vessels. Construction then took the form of stretching existing ships.

THE INAUGURAL VOYAGES

The official opening of business was June 15, 1960, but the day prior, with Captain Paddy Hannigan at the helm, *M.V. Sidney* set sail with a cargo of press and dignitaries. The June 14 pre-inaugural voyage started off after days of rain. Swartz Bay terminal, still under construction, was a mudhole. The guests climbed aboard for a happy party and a trip to Tsawwassen and back. Upon her return, the ship cracked against a partially complete wing wall and a mess of creosote dumped all over then-reporter, and subsequent Member of Parliament, Simma Holt.

The next day brought a rush of curious passengers from both sides of Georgia Strait, predictable confusion and more than one incident. "It wouldn't stop raining. We were in mud up to our knees at Swartz Bay," Monty Aldous recalls. At Tsawwassen, the best story was created by Elmer Leard, whose McKenzie Tug and Barge Company had moved the gigantic tonnage of rocks for the causeway. Leard called Aldous the day before to ask how he might become the first paying passenger out of Tsawwassen. "I told him I wouldn't pull any strings," Aldous said. But Leard was determined. He arrived at

Her Majesty's innauguaral is welcomed by Prince Rupert's fishing fleet.

DONUT DENNY

Fame can arrive from bizarre directions. As the enterprise at Swartz Bay terminal thrived, a smooth-talking salesman from Vancouver's Hole-in-One Donut Company sold an electronic donut-making machine to the terminal cafeteria. The lady cooks quickly attracted rave reviews for the assortment of coconut, sugar and nut coated donuts they produced. Their boss, terminal agent Denny Keen, was so impressed that his kitchen soon began supplying all the vessels running to Tsawwassen and the Gulf Islands.

The production line at the Swartz Bay Ferry Terminal and Donut Bakery soon topped 1,000 donuts a day, neatly sent to the ships in boxes of four dozen. The Horseshoe Bay, Nanaimo and Sunshine Coast ships were not so fortunate. Their donuts came from a commercial bakery. When a private industry strike prevented delivery to northern routes, Keen and his ladies expanded their market, offering to supply all BC Ferries routes. The striking union wailed to the press about "strike breaking," shouting the word "scab." The cover was blown and Keen was forever after dubbed "Donut Denny." When he took his pension a few years ago, the donut business was phased out, much like the sports tradition of retiring a star's number.

the terminal in the pre-dawn hours, becoming the first in the queue and, ultimately, the first paying car on the ship. When they reached Swartz Bay, Leard jumped into his vehicle, nosed squarely against the loading door, and proceeded to break off his ignition key in the lock. No one else could move. He had to be towed off the ship.

The ships' food and service attracted rave reviews. Aldous remembers that the economy and, more importantly, the morale of Victoria were instantly uplifted. Hotel managers had only one complaint. They were grateful for the room trade, but most of their business customers were eating on the ships.

Aldous said the ship design had only one flaw. The top deck cafeteria proved far too small for the demand. The engineers were instructed to discuss remedies with the shipyards and it was decided that a large pre-fabricated dining room could be dropped into place at the aft end of the main deck. Aldous' problem was selling the idea to W.A.C. Bennett.

He waited for an occasion when the premier would be traveling on the ships. When the day arrived, Aldous joined Bennett and quickly escorted him to a stateroom. At the right moment, just when the heavy overflow crowd at the cafeteria was beginning to get ugly, the general manager suggested that the premier might like to have something to eat. Bennett was amazed at both the crowd and the mood, just as he noticed an old friend from Kelowna. Aldous said the friend couldn't have performed better. He called to the premier,

"Great ship, Cec, but you could starve to death!" The new dining rooms were soon approved and fixed in place.

Passenger demand was so brisk that two more ships were ordered, slightly broader at the beam and with many improvements based on experience. When *M.V. City of Vancouver* and *M.V. City of Victoria* entered the fleet, an hourly service became possible on the route.

FAREWELL TO COMPETITION

Captain Alex Peabody and Captain Harry Terry remained close advisors to Bennett throughout the early days, but political pressure was coming from Nanaimo and points served by the northern route about the inadequacy of service from Black Ball. Premier Bennett asked Peabody to make improvements, but, now fighting the impressive first class ships on the southern route and the embarrassment of media comparisons, the Black Ball boss was having a difficult financial time.

The government was in the ferry business to stay. On September 1, 1961, it purchased the entire operation of Gavin Mouat's Gulf Islands Ferries for $249,823, with a pledge of better service. The deal added four small vessels to the BC Ferries system.

Bennett started negotiations with Peabody, and in November a $6,690,000 deal brought howls of protest from the media. The Toronto *Globe and Mail* charged that British Columbia was "suffocating the company (Black Ball) with taxpayers' money." The ships were ridiculed. Few observers understood that the vessels were the smallest part of the deal, useless without the Nanaimo, Horseshoe Bay, Langdale and Jervis Inlet terminals owned by Peabody.

With the exceptions of the modern *Chinook II,* and the amazing fifty-eight-year-old *Kahloke,* BC Ferries had acquired only headaches. The old *Smokwa,* once a Halifax harbor ferry was the last steam-powered ferry on the North American west coast. When ladies walked on the wooden deck of *Bainbridge,* high heels frequently poked right through the floorboards. *Quillayute* wasn't much better. Frank Ramsay remembers a time when *Smokwa* crashed heavily

into the Horseshoe Bay terminal causing sufficient damage to retire for the day. He says he walked up to the bridge and while there, casually looked into the radar scope. He did a doubletake when he saw a girlie picture pasted over the screen inside. When questioned, the captain said, "Oh the radar hasn't worked for weeks. We thought we'd give them something to look at."

The next day, *Smokwa* was back on the Langdale run when a piston blew and tugs were called. By the time the tow was hitched, *Kahloke* had passed her three times, back and forth on the route. Because *Smokwa* was still required to help move all the cars, passengers were urged to drive aboard and be towed. Many flatly refused.

Despite problems, the complete northern ship system—ships, terminals, an operating company and complete staff—could not have been acquired any other way and likely not at any less cost. The unionized staff concerned Aldous, but he says it worked out well. "To my absolute delight, the people up there enthusiastically were competing, trying to be better."

THE POLITICAL CLIMATE

Relations between Monty Aldous and W.A.C. Bennett remained on a mutual and formal "Mister" basis for many years, but it became a special friendship. At the outset, the general manager announced that he intended to run the company like a private business. Bennett greeted the statement with an enigmatic smile and commented, "Most of the way, but remember you are dealing with the public and the public's money." But Bennett was always there with finances, commitment, and the support needed for independence from politics.

At first, politics was the toughest part of Aldous' job. "One of the greatest difficulties was thinking like a businessman on the one hand, but also thinking about the politics at the same time," Aldous said.

When members of the Legislature would try to gain special privilege, head office officials were always suspicious that the politically-appointed executive, Ron Worley, was somehow involved. After pressure from an MLA on one occasion, in an attempt to get a friend hired, Aldous went to the premier. "He told me to hire the best people and said, 'I will go one step further. . .if any of our people *are* the best people, don't hire them.' "

One day Phil Gaglardi arrived at Swartz Bay toll booth and the cashier failed to recognize him. Days later, the terminal agent received a photo of the highways minister along with a stern Gaglardi rebuke, "The next person who fails to recognize me is going to be fired."

Another day, assistant general manager Ron Worley was in his car when he heard on the radio that the price of coffee on the ferries was going up from ten cents to twenty. He was outraged. He phoned the office demanding to know if the story was true. No one who knew about the matter was around at the time. Worley spoke on the phone to engineer Sandy Ritchie and finally said he was going to tell the editor of the *Vancouver Sun* that the price of coffee had not gone up Ritchie recalls asking him, "You're going out on a limb, aren't you?" Worley replied that he had just been on the ferry and he didn't pay twenty cents. He made the denial to the newspapers, and he was widely quoted. The problem was that the price increase was a fact. Only later did Worley remember that he had been given a free cup of coffee on the ship.

University of British Columbia researchers would help create one of the better Worley tales. A group of them studying the habits of seagulls, decided to dye a number of the birds with a pink color. The sample gulls became easy to spot for research purposes and a small newspaper story advised the public. Worley must have missed the story. One day on the bridge of a ship approaching Active Pass, he spotted the pink seagulls, exclaiming his discovery to the ferry officers. In fine deadpan form, the captain told his visitor, "That's because pink shrimp are so plentiful in this area, and the gulls eat so many of them." The next day, at head office, there were hoots of laughter when Worley seriously announced his amazing discovery. Ron Worley stepped down as Assistant General Manager of BC Ferries in 1967, moving to the government's travel industry department as deputy minister.

"The Admiral" at rest aboard the fleet.

W.A.C. Bennett's son Bill, British Columbia premier since 1975, remembers a particular beef his father had during the early days. "He would wince every time he heard a British accent over a terminal public address system." Although a loyal supporter of the commonwealth, the Crown and the British public, W.A.C. Bennett would think of political ramifications. Bill Bennett recalls that his father would sometimes mutter, "Why can't they find any Canadians?" When anything other than a British accent was heard at the terminals, W.A.C. was suspicious that some actor was kept around for days the premier was listening. The reason for the dominance of British-born personnel within the company at the beginning, and, to some extent, through promotions and seniority into the present, was merely a reflection of the provincial shipping industry of the day. These were the best people available to fill the jobs.

On a more serious note, Monty Aldous remembers Bennett as a rock of strength. "He liked a good debate if no one else was present. If you made your point, he would not only approve, he would back you to the hilt."

THE GRAND OLD LADY

She was the pride of New York harbor when Asbury Park, *with her speed of 20 knots, arrived from Philadelphia shipyards to challenge her peers in 1903. But no domestic ship could match her speed or comfort. However in her 15 years connecting New York and New Jersey, there were also complaints. She was too large to properly maneuver in the tight channels and crowded lanes of the harbor and she created sufficient wash to upset the waters of sedate local beaches.*

In 1919, Asbury Park *journeyed via Panama to San Francisco for extensive renovations, conversion from coal to oil and to begin a quarter century of service in the Bay area. In 1925 she was renamed* City of Sacramento.

The ship was sold to Captain Alexander Peabody's Puget Sound Navigation Company of Seattle just before the United States entered World War II. However, before she could be transferred to the Pacific Northwest, the government requisitioned her to transport shipyard workers across San Francisco Bay. She was finally towed to Seattle through a harrowing series of storms and frequent lay-bys, entering service from Seattle to Bremerton in 1944. In 1948, she was laid up by her owners, after the State of Washington purchased most of Peabody's fleet. In 1951, Captain Alexander Peabody moved three ships and the Black Ball Line to British Columbia.

One of these, City of Sacramento, *went into drydock at Yarrows in Victoria for extensive refit, emerging in splendid condition as* M.V. Kahloke. *She was still in the Black Ball fleet and still serving with distinction when the B.C. government took over Black Ball in 1961 and at the age of 60 in 1963, she was renamed* Langdale Queen.

On July 23, 1976, her days of passenger shipping ended. Maritime historian Frank A. Clapp described the scene. "With signal flags flying and long rust stains streaking her paintwork, Langdale Queen *quietly slipped away from the Horseshoe Bay terminal." She was to enter a rather ignominious era. BC Ferries, conscious of her heritage, sold her for $50,000, much less than her scrap value, to Vancouver entrepreneurs. They renamed the ship* Lady Grace, *and then recouped their entire investment by selling the engines. Plans to create a Vancouver harbor restaurant on the top decks and a marine service center below, soon soured. One day she was found sunk at her berth. Police suspected, but were unable to prove, sabotage. After finally being raised from the mud,* Langdale Queen *has been moored at a series of storage berths for years. In mid-1985 she sat forlornly on the north shore of eastern Vancouver harbor.*

From the top, as Asbury Park *(1903),* City of Sacramento *(1925),* Kahloke *(1951) and, as* Langdale Queen *(1962), her retirement in 1976 ended 73 years of distinguished service.*

MONTY– THE LIBERAL

Historians may find it odd that the late Jimmy Sinclair, cabinet minister in the government of Prime Minister Louis St. Laurent, west coast Liberal of considerable power and frequent political nemesis of W.A.C. Bennett, made at least one significant contribution to Social Credit success. He recommended the man who would guide BC Ferries through their glory years of growth.

In late 1959, the ships and terminals of the new BC Ferries operation were rapidly taking shape and the government was looking for a manager. The position was nationally advertised, but no applicants appealed to the government. W.A.C. Bennett was consulting his long-time friend, Captain Harry Terry of Northland Navigation, and Captain Alexander Peabody of Black Ball Ferries while, in North Vancouver, Monty Aldous was pondering whether or not to apply. He consulted not only his employer at B.C. Packers, but also Jimmy Sinclair, a political associate. They all urged him to go after the job. When Aldous' application finally arrived in Victoria, Cap' Terry lifted it to the top of the pile, scrawling across the bottom of the page, "Jimmy Sinclair's campaign manager!" He then forwarded it to W.A.C. Bennett with the recommendation that this was the man for the job.

After youthful years in logging camps and fisheries up and down the coast, Aldous returned to Vancouver in 1941. He spent eighteen years managing warehouses and, for several more years the ships of B.C. Packers. Active in North Vancouver community work, he served a term as a municipal alderman. Aldous became national president of the Junior Chamber of Commerce in 1954, completing a two-year term.

Aldous says he was at first uncertain whether or not the government should be in the ferry business, but soon became excited by the challenge. Finally, he was convinced that no one but the government could deliver the standard of service required. In December 1959, he reached an agreement with the government to manage the venture. Years afterward in the British Columbia Legislature, any time the opposition raised the spectre of "patronage" in the Bennett government, the premier would rise in the full flower of wounded dignity, and remind the House that it was he who had hired "Jimmy Sinclair's man" to run the BC Ferries.

THE ORIGINAL 89

It was a grand occasion on June 15, 1970 when 89 original employees of the British Columbia Ferries gathered for dinner at Victoria's Hollyrood House. On day one of the government ferry service, 191 employees were in place. A decade later, 89 were still playing a vital role in the affairs of the company. They became known on this 10th anniversary as "The Original 89," shortened in BC Ferries colloquialism to "An Original." Many of them were still active on the 25th anniversary in 1985.

At the anniversary dinner, the large Chinese contingent was led by Bill Lowe and Don Eng. Captains B.G.K. Owen-Jones (M.V. Tsawwassen) and John Callan (M.V. Sidney), who had commanded the maiden voyages, were among the seafaring group along with the first Chief Engineer, O.H. Henriksen and his staff. Frank Ramsay and Denny Keen, instrumental in terminal development, were on hand, as were key early sales, marketing and traffic people, including Bob Innes and Dave Price. Maria Logan, who had joined the company as a secretary at Burrard Drydock before the first passenger paid a fare, attended and became the only female "Original." Monty Aldous, Bill Weston and Captain Peter de Cunha led the executive brigade.

On a beautiful evening at Tsawwassen on May 28, 1985, Queen of the North leisurely sailed for a Gulf Islands cruise, a 25th-anniversary reenactment of the 1970 dinner. Top executives of the company presented Founders' Plaques and specially struck pins to 57 of the "Original 89" who were able to attend. Some of their colleagues had died during the interval, some were incapacitated, and some lived elsewhere, but one veteran guessed that of the 57 who attended the jubilant Queen of the North dinner cruise, 40 percent were still active on the payroll.

A highlight of the evening was the unveiling of a large bronze bust of the company's first general manager, Monty F. Aldous, meticulously created by prominent Ottawa artist Harold Pfeiffer. It is a permanent fixture in the foyer of the British Columbia Ferry Corporation head office.

A BLIZZARD OF CONSTRUCTION

While head office raced through growing pains, and the public controversy swirled around the takeover of Black Ball in the north, the main actions remained in the shipyards of the south. With the expanding fleet and the diversity of names, Premier Bennett asked Aldous if he had any suggestions. The general manager thought for a moment and pointed out that CP called all its ships *Princesses.* "Our ships are much better than theirs so why don't we call ours *Queens?*" It appealed to Bennett's sense of humor and the policy struck: major ships would be *Queen of* and the minor vessels would have the *Queen* trailing their name.

Sidney and *Tsawwassen,* along with *City of Vancouver* and *City of Victoria* were immediately changed and were soon followed by the *Queens of Saanich, Esquimalt, Nanaimo, New Westminster* and *Burnaby.* In 1963 a smaller, purpose built vessel of a Quebec design, never popular with engineers, joined the fleet to connect the mainland and the Gulf Islands. She was *Queen of the Islands.* Three small inter-islands vessels were built for about $1 million each in 1965: *Bowen Queen, Powell River Queen* and *Mayne Queen.*

The greatest excitement, particularly for Premier W.A.C. Bennett, came in 1966, with the construction of a combination cruise ship and ferry to link Prince Rupert to the south. *Queen of Prince Rupert,* with a large live aboard crew, was to be the flagship of the fleet. Although Captain Terry might have been accused of trying to avoid competition for his Northland Navigation, he predicted "a sea of red ink." It was one time Bennett refused to listen and, in fact, the northern service has consistently lost money. It has, however, played a crucial role in tying the province together.

The Susie Q arrived via the Panama Canal from Quebec, the only important ship in the company's history not built in local shipyards, other than those acquired from Black Ball. The double-ender, *Pere Nouvel,* a 172-car, 725 passenger ferry, was too good a deal to pass up. Christened *Sunshine Coast Queen* she soon became a local landmark, but her heavy hull, for Great Lakes icebreaking, made her a fuel gobbler all her days.

As the new ships entered the fleet, BC Ferries was able to retire the worst of the Black Ball problems, although *Chinook II* and *Kahloke* were to serve for years with distinction, renamed *Sechelt Queen* and *Langdale Queen* respectively. The renaming of *Chinook II* was to produce a spark of outrage from W.A.C. Bennett. When Monty Aldous proposed naming her "Gibsons Queen," the premier snapped, "That's a terrible idea. Can't you see the Gordon Gibson (a prominent Liberal opponent) jokes!"

Black Ball veteran Gerry Barber, now superintendent of all terminals, recalls the first day a modern BC Ferries ship rounded the point into Horseshoe Bay.

"We thought she was the *Queen Elizabeth,*" he said.

THE PURPLE EMPIRE
CHAPTER FIVE

Passenger shipping companies use either colors or special insignia with an officer's stripes to indicate his department or specialty: navy blue between the gold braid for captains and deck officers; white for the purser's service staff; green for the radio room and red for the medical people. The considerable domain of the four-striped chief engineer is the world of purple or mauve.

The BC Ferries engineering shrine, Deas Dock, was built on the site of the George Massey Tunnel construction headquarters. Huge concrete tunnel sections were off-loaded at a Fraser River temporary berth. Today it has evolved into the envy of global shipping—an "in-house" service facility and parts repository capable of almost every ferry repair except drydocking. Up to three vessels can be comfortably accommodated at any one time in the Deas Dock lagoon.

Although ferry engineering has a low profile, it has been a major force from the outset, consistently attracting the most attention from industry professionals. In a jaded moment, one captain, convinced that the company's passion for engineering had become unhealthy, dubbed the Deas establishment, "The Purple Empire."

The signature of sea power is the weight of braid.

| MASTER | CHIEF ENGINEER | CHIEF OFFICER | 2nd ENGINEER | 2nd OFFICER | 3rd ENGINEER | JUNIOR ENGINEER | CHIEF STEWARD |

THE BEGINNING

On Valentine's Day 1960, eight engineers were hired. Four were posted at Burrard Drydock on the mainland and four at Victoria Machinery Depot. They would conduct the sea trials and engine tests. This was the group, under engineering and construction boss Bill Weston, that would win BC Ferries its greatest professional acclaim.

As the fleet came together, headaches piled upon headaches. A spare parts inventory was assembled at Tsawwassen Terminal even before the first ship sailed, but the new vessels remained largely dependent upon their builders' shipyards for any major repairs. Engineers did most of their work aboard ship, and with both of the first vessels necessary to maintain schedule, the work would frequently have to take place after hours, sometimes shuttling over to the nearby Fraser River dock at Deas Tunnel.

Complications multiplied with the addition of Gulf Islands Ferries small vessels and the diverse fleet of the Black Ball Line in 1961. There were almost as many different engines as ships, all requiring unique replacement parts and specialized technical skills. The engineers who came with their vessels to BC Ferries were frequently the only ones who could repair them.

The company aggravated these problems when the next four new ships were constructed. *M.V. City of Victoria* and *M.V. City of Vancouver* brought a shift from the dependable Mirrlees Twins engine aboard *M.V. Tsawwassen* and *M.V. Sidney* to Paxman Twins, on the basis of a lower tender price. After the Paxmans quickly proved themselves problematic, Fairbanks Morse engines were bought for *Queen of Saanich* and *Queen of Esquimalt*. According to one executive, they were chosen "because they allegedly were constructed in Canada." This was later discovered to be a ruse. The engines were merely assembled in Canada and proved to be little better than the Paxmans. Describing the Paxman and Fairbanks experiences, one senior engineer said, "They had every bloody problem you could think of."

In addition to the obviously confused engineering inherited from Gulf Islands Ferries and Black Ball, the six new ships of BC Ferries constructed between 1960 and 1963 offered three separate engines. By late 1962, the company was in desperate need of someone to coordinate engineering procedures, standardize machinery and develop a sophisticated service facility. They found their man in Levis, Quebec.

The original Mirrlees diesels, the heart of BC Ferries engineering.

GEORGE BALDWIN

At sixteen, George Baldwin started in the shipping business at the then-preeminent shipyards of Clydeside in Scotland. When he was twenty-one, he went to sea in the engine rooms of the Blue Funnel Line. One of his dreams was to visit British Columbia, where his tradesman uncle had emigrated in 1906. However, his seven-year seafaring career took him everywhere in the world but British Columbia.

Tiring of life at sea and anxious to spend time with his family, Baldwin left ship at Hong Kong to become building superintendent for one of the world's largest banks, *The Honkers and Shankers,* the Hong Kong and Shanghai Banking Corporation. For three years this was his shore-based career. He might still be there were it not for the wives of British banking executives who believed it was his highest daily priority to repair their household appliances.

After a six-month leave from Hong Kong, George Baldwin finally came to Canada, albeit the wrong coast, in 1959. He landed a position as superintendant engineer with the Saint John Shipbuilding and Drydock Company and the world of Kenneth Colin Irving. A better financial opportunity came in 1962 and he moved the family to Levis, Quebec, where he became instantly unhappy in the different culture of French Canada. His eyes once again turned to the West Coast. Following the dramatic activities of the government of British Columbia in the shipping business, he was quick to respond to their advertisement for an engineering suprintendant.

THE CHIEF OF ENGINEERS

"I couldn't believe there were so many different engines. . . . I wondered what kind of a madman put this fleet together."—George Baldwin, General Manager, BC Ferries, referring to his initial thoughts in 1962

When this wirey Scot who is currently general manager of the corporation began his duties as engineering superintendant in December 1962, he was both astonished and terrified by the diversity of the fleet. "I couldn't even figure out how many ships they had, with all the name changes and the various companies coming together," George Baldwin remembers. The mixed bag of vessels from Black Ball and Gulf Ferries rarely had two engines in common, and even the six new specially designed ships, in place when Baldwin arrived, had three different engine plants.

It was his job to organize all maintenance, spare parts and servicing procedures and to supervise the activities of the chief engineers aboard ship. By mid-1962, BC Ferries was in desperate need of this supervisory engineering assistance. Growth had been explosive and chaotic. Ship engineers were looking after the vessels in an ad hoc way. Bill Weston, the marine superintendant, was trying to supervise both maintenance and new construction.

Weston and Monty Aldous flew back to Montreal in November 1962 to interview the short list of four final applicants. Drydock experience was the most essential credential. Baldwin was the second of two morning interviewees, and the others were planned for the afternoon. At noon, Aldous received an urgent phone call from Vancouver—the main terminal at Tsawwassen had been destroyed by fire. Aldous asked Weston to stay and handle the afternoon interviews while he caught the next flight to Vancouver. "However, I told Bill that as far as I was concerned, we had our man," Aldous said.

George Baldwin served as engineering superintendant until 1981 when he was promoted to general manager. He has since been elected president of one of shipping's most prestigious organizations, the International Marine Transit Association, for a term commencing October 1985. This is not only a personal tribute but also one indicative of the high esteem British Columbia Ferry Corporation enjoys within the global shipping industry.

SOPHISTICATION

With the arrival of Baldwin under the supervision of Bill Weston, one of the world's most self-contained, innovative and cost effective in-house engineering systems began to evolve. The engineering superintendent's first office was a tiny affair at Tsawwassen Terminal but soon after, BC Ferries was able to spin off some space from the Department of Highways at the Deas facility, and the purple empire began.

New ship construction came to a temporary halt by late 1966, with the launching of *Queen of Prince Rupert*. But the greatest engineering achievements—the ones that would raise the eyebrows of the international shipping community—occurred through adaptation of existing ships. During the mid-1960s, platform decks were installed inside the car decks of nine ships. The new galleries raised capacity from 106 to 150 cars.

But passenger demand and traffic growth were relentless. No sooner had that project been completed, when plans were made to "stretch" the ships—a relatively rare procedure at the time. When BC Ferries told insurers and Canada Steamship Inspectors that it planned to cut seven vessels in half and then weld into place new 84-foot midsections, they said it couldn't be done. It took a serious engineering study and evidence of precedent elsewhere to convince the inspectors that the structure of the ships would not be weakened. Capacity was increased to 192 cars for all seven ships by 1972.

Many of the engineering experiments have been far less glamorous, but equally intriguing. When the floating bridge was finally opened at Kelowna crossing Okanagan Lake during the early 1960s, the ferry *Lloyd Jones* became available. Virtually identical to *Saltspring Queen*, it was thought that the 32-car vessel would be ideal to connect Crofton to Vancouver Island, with Vesuvius on Salt Spring Island. Engineers pondered how to transport the ferry. She was ultimately cut into sections, transported on flatbed trucks, and

Three ships are shown in the Deas Dock lagoon (opposite page) in 1966. The in-house service centre evolved under the direction of longtime engineering superintendent and current general manager George Baldwin (opposite right).

pieced back together to emerge as *Bowen Queen,* and, subsequently, *Vesuvius Queen.*

Construction of three jumbo super ferries during the mid-1970s, and two more in 1981, dramatically expanded the fleet. However the company's most impressive engineering feat occurred at the outset of the 1980s. Four ships were substantially enlarged. This time the slice was linear. Heavy jacks lifted the vessels apart and extra decks were jammed into the middle. The capacity grew to 400 cars for two of these *Victoria-class* or "V" class ships and 284 for the other two (fewer cars left room for more overheight vehicles). They all received new engines at the time. Powerful MAK engines from Germany which had proven so successful aboard the new jumbo ships of the 1970s, finally were installed aboard the enlarged *Queens of Victoria, Vancouver, Saanich* and *Esquimalt,* to replace the problematic Paxman and Fairbanks Morse originals.

A cartoonist in a BC Ferries staff publication once described the reshaping of ships with the caption, "If I stretch it any more, it'll become a bridge."

SHORE FACILITIES

Engineering advances in the company have gone far beyond the ships themselves. Terminal development formerly took place under the Ministry of Highways but is now exclusively under the Deas Dock umbrella. The most modern of these on the main routes rival the comfort of airports, although a future challenge will be to get foot-passengers closer to the ships.

Ship turn-around time is the crucial foundation of efficient ferry transport, and, for over two decades, it's been acknowledged that no one has ever done it faster than BC Ferries. Delays not only annoy the public, but the cost in fuel and manpower is significant. The large ships of the 70s forced heavy terminal construction to permit simultaneous top and bottom loading and the facilities are expected to expand in the future.

THE PAINT SHOP

Mixed feelings prevailed throughout the province in 1984 when the decision was made to repaint the entire BC Ferries fleet. The historic pastel blues of the Dogwood Fleet would gradually yield to the lively red, white and blue standardized color program for all provincial government services. Some critics suggested it was a needless expense.

In fact, it was no expense at all. Paint Master Don Stephens and his crew at Deas have done all painting, signing and decorative assignments for the company since the earliest days. Since every ship is repainted every two years, the change of color was meaningless. (Repainting, before the era of restraint, used to be an annual affair.)

The sporty, fresh new colors soon won approval from most people both inside and outside the company. Some observers see the government's "BC Spirit," flag symbol—now attached to all the ships—as clearly political, but one BC Ferries seaman was thinking only of aesthetics as he commented, "Wouldn't it have been terrible if the NDP had decided to repaint the fleet in their colors?" It was a reference to the orange and black colors of the official opposition, the New Democractic Party.

The Paint Shop at Deas regularly repaints all the ships. The recent task has been a complete new color scheme, including the Expo 86 stacks. It's not a flawless operation. These chaps found that the giant "Q" looked different from afar.

79

INFLATABLE LIFE RAFTS

Among the facilities at Deas Dock is the largest inflatable life raft servicing center in the world. It too was an early BC Ferries innovation. Amid the construction blitz of the early 1960s, the decision was made that the large fabric rafts would be the backbone of safety planning. Traditional lifeboats for a large passenger manifest, with a relatively small crew to manage them, would be impractical.

The United Kingdom suppliers of the best inflatable rafts salivated not only about the sales prospects to the mushrooming BC Ferries fleet, but at the required and profitable on-going service contracts. But Monty Aldous called their bluff. He demanded that BC Ferries be permitted to service the inflatables itself and that the supplier train company personnel to a level of proficiency that would satisfy Canadian government safety inspectors. His alternative was another manufacturer. The British reluctantly complied.

"We were the major buyer of inflatable rafts in the world, and we soon became the largest and the best servicing center," Aldous said. As the system developed, tradesmen from around the world came to British Columbia to learn the techniques.

The inflatable rafts are substantial 25-passenger crafts, complete with tent coverings to protect from the elements. In 1985, there were 996 in the fleet, each valued at $5,500. Completely outfitted with emergency supplies, the total price tag rises to $8,300—a fleet inventory of $8.3 million.

Every raft goes through vigorous annual testing and it receives safety certification from transport inspectors. They are routinely replaced. A novice would consider the rejected rafts to be in perfectly good condition.

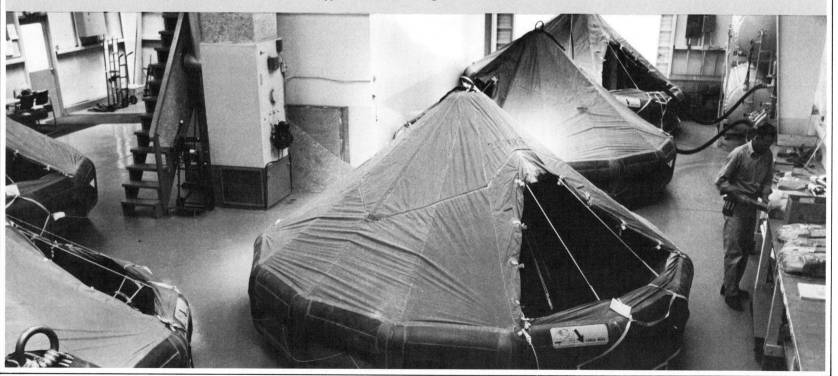

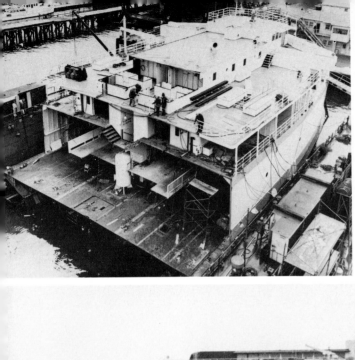

As the company prepared to celebrate its 10th anniversary in 1970, a bold plan to slice and stretch the seven ships went into effect. Welded into place were 84-foot midsections, adding capacity for 42 more cars on each ship, and proportionately more lounge space. The photos show the vessels' component parts being sliced, and the new midsection being towed into place. The photo at the centre displays the elogated ship before being repainted.

81

The Victoria-Class, or "V"-Class ships were born in 1981, with the addition of a complete new car deck. Queen of Esquimalt *(right), originally built to carry 106 cars, now accommodates 400.*

The lifting of Victoria, Vancouver, Saanich *and* Esquimalt *was likely the boldest chapter in a history of perpetual engineering innovation. As the photos show, the ships were sliced horizontally along their circumferance. Welded into place on the lower car decks, were 129 giant hydraulic jacks per vessel. When the cut was complete, these were meticulously employed in unison to separate the decks. The new car decks and support beams were then inserted.*

The four ships emerged identical to size, although, with extra platform decks, the Queens of Saanich *and* Esquimalt *can carry 400 cars. The Van and The Vic, with extra room left for overheights, can accommodate 284 vehicles.*

Cartoonist Len Norris and others have publicly wondered what BC Ferries might come up with next, in the passion for jamming extra cars onto existing ships.

Artist David O. Thorne's drawing follows the life of Queen of Victoria *from her original size when launched in 1962, stretched by 84 feet in 1970, and lifted to house an extra car deck in 1981.*

Terminal maintenance and development have been as difficult a construction assignment as the more glamorous shipbuilding. In fact, at the outset of the company, the choice of locations was far more controversial then any ship or route decision ever made. Until recent times, when it became a fully integrated component of BC Ferries, terminal matters were handled directly by the Highways Department, in cooperation with the ferry fleet.

Deas Dock Superintendent, Ted Dodds, said that the inventory of spare parts in his domain, including a sea of massive replacement propellers, is valued at approximately $7 million. Inside one of the main buildings is a large chart showing the immediate location of each ship, including the regular rotation of vessels at Deas for either routine servicing or major repairs. Delivery trucks are dispatched daily with supplies, spare parts or any other requirements to meet the ships at the appropriate terminal.

Perhaps the only industry observers who don't marvel at the self-sufficiency of BC Ferries are the major local drydock companies, which have, over the years, played a leading role in building the fleet. They built the ships and did much of the servicing, but Deas Dock has almost eliminated them. Burrard Drydock does little more now but scrape down the hull bottoms and even that has been reduced by the application of an expensive new "no-stick" paint, SPC (self-polishing copolymer).

Ken Shaw, the assistant foreman of the Deas Dock machine shop, said other drydocks are at a severe competitive disadvantage. He said they have 12 separate unionized trades, while Deas has just one union and a great deal of job flexibility. "We are all very versatile in our own fields."

NO RESPECT

Shipping engineers throughout the world share the same frustration and the same joy of being independent. They are the only ones who understand what they do and what they say. Company executives and even masters, when they walk through engine rooms, give chief engineers thoughtful nods as various points are explained. The engineer might just as well speak the ancient and lost language of the Etruscans.

BC Ferries fine staff magazine, *The Dolphin,* featured a lengthy story about the conversion of *Queen of the North* in 1979. The article talked about the giant 16-cylinder KA-ME-WA engines. A month later, exasperated company engineering manager Jim Watson wrote the editor to express appreciation for the attention. He pointed out, however, that KA-ME-WA made the ship's propellers, not the engines.

THE GENTLEMEN OF GREASE

This story from Britain's PUNCH *magazine pays tribute to ships' engineers.*

"It was the last night before the S.S. Magnifico *docked at Southampton, England. Celeste de Vigne, wrapped in black chantilly lace, with a parure of sapphires glittering in her bosom, entered the first class dining room, trying not to feel overwhelmed by the singular honor accorded her. She had delayed her entrance deliberately. Now a hundred pair of eyes followed her as she glided to that social Holy of Holies—the Engineer's Table—with its beau monde of Archdukes, Rajahs, Grand Viziers, Serene Highnesses and pretenders. Celeste* knew that the Captain of S.S. Magnifico was not among them—he was holding petty court of Wall Street riffraff in an unconsidered corner.

"As Celeste neared her goal, great men of two continents rose smiling in her honor. The Chief Engineer, a thickset Caledonian with hardly an oil smear to denote his proud calling, his fingernails but lightly grimed, stepped forward to kiss her hand. Celeste's heart fluttered like a trapped dove. Then she realized the Chief Engineer was speaking to her, indicating a chair.

" 'Celeste,' he said, in the cultivated accents of his native Lanarkshire, 'pit your airse doon there.' "

THE
MECHANICAL CZAR

William B. Weston sometimes operated with all the charm of a Caterpillar D-9 bulldozer. A pugnacious shipping engineer, he, more than anyone else, built the physical plant of the system, astonishing the world as one ship after another rolled down the slips into service. Nothing happened in ship construction or engineering that didn't cross his desk. Dynamic, determined and a tireless worker, Weston demanded and received the same dedication from both engineers and outside contractors. It was eminently simple. They either performed or they were gone.

A veteran of Britain's Royal Electrical Mechanical Engineers and Canada's northern shipping industry, Bill Weston came aboard with Monty Aldous by order-in-council on January 2, 1960. Within a month, he had hired eight chief engineers. Originally marine superintendant, Weston was elevated to assistant general manager in 1967. While the focal point of his efforts always remained with construction and engineering, his dominant bearing asserted itself in all company activities.

At the height of Weston's power, a seaman found a unique way of catching the executive's attention. Weston one day arrived on a ship's bridge and he introduced himself to everyone. The seaman asked, "Are you any relation to that joker who is screwing everything up in Victoria?"

Although his contribution to the company development was extraordinary, Weston's departure from the scene was a sad event. The New Democratic Party government (1972-1975) decided to replace Monty Aldous with an outsider. Weston felt he was next in line for the job, so he promptly resigned from the company. However, few executive colleagues believed his nature suited the top job. As much as they admired Weston's technical work, they unanimously stated that his blunt, brusque bearing, with little apparent sensitivity towards others cost him the control of BC Ferries.

Part of the $7 million permanent repository of spare parts at Deas Dock, is a veritable battalion of replacement propellers.

CHAPTER SIX

"At first, the general public was against it (government ferries)...
I thought it was an immortal dead level cinch,"—Captain J.V. Bell
Jr.

Controversy over route change is not unique. Almost every time a
change is announced, a maelstrom of public wrangling follows.

The sedate village of Horseshoe Bay almost went to war in 1953
when Black Ball Ferries proposed making it the terminus for
Vancouver Island service. "If the Black Ball people are permitted to
run a service out of Horseshoe Bay, their next move might be to
institute services out of Horseshoe Bay to Victoria, Prince Rupert
and Alaska," the ratepayers' association protested at the time. They
decried the probability that one of Canada's best fishing coves would
be destroyed. However, the Black Ball Line overcame opposition,
the route to Nanaimo thrived and the commerce of Horseshoe Bay
parallelled ferry development.

BC Ferries has never been happy, though, with the Horseshoe
Bay—Departure Bay (Nanaimo) routing. At 30-nautical miles in
length, it is far more costly to serve than the 24-nautical mile gap
between Tsawwassen and Swartz Bay. As well, meeting the schedules
has consistently been a more difficult problem on this northern trunk
route.

From earliest days, route planners have cast longing eyes on
Gabriola Island as the sensible stepping stone for ferry service. One
of the most costly aspects of construction would be a major bridge
connecting it with Vancouver Island. The company ran into a storm
of protest from Gabriola Island residents before deciding on the
expensive upgrading of the Trans Canada Highway and the Horseshoe Bay terminal. They complained that the environment of the
island would be destroyed and that traffic would soon overpopulate
their blissful surroundings. At one point, Monty Aldous, half-joking,
suggested to W.A.C. Bennett that they build a terminal on Gabriola
connected with an express, fenced-off highway, and bridge direct to
Vancouver Island. There would be no access to Gabriola from the
route and the islanders would be protected from too much traffic. "I
knew that within a year the Gabriola residents would be clamoring
to have the fence knocked down to make their ferry transport more

convenient," Aldous said. But nothing came of it.

In more recent years, it has been accepted that the main route from Horseshoe Bay to Nanaimo is here to stay. However, studies have suggested the possiblity of a so-called "third crossing," from the mainland near the mouth of the Fraser River to points on Gabriola and Valdes Islands, as well as Yellow Point and Duke Point south of Nanaimo. On the Vancouver side, the studies looked at using either the existing terminal at Tsawwassen or a completely new facility at Iona, just off Point Grey (a much shorter route). A 1983 study estimated that total development costs for all the route variations ranged from a low $68 million (Yellow Point—Tsawwassen), to a high of $164 million (Valdes South - Tsawwassen), including all bridges, highways and terminals.

Planners have made traffic projections into the future. Because the capacities of both major routes will be saturated by 1998, they've concluded that by the early 1990s, serious consideration will have to be given to a third crossing. They project a construction period of five years.

CAPTAIN JAMES VALENTINE BELL JR.

Jimmy Bell, or *Dinger* as his wartime air force colleagues called him, is one of those larger-than-life figures that color the pages of west coast history. He served the BC Ferries from day one until his retirement in June 1982, first as mate, but predominantly as master, charming and entertaining everyone in his path for twenty-two years. Everything happened to Jimmy.

"Jimmy Bell could do things with ships that none of us could do—or would do," a fellow officer remembers with a grin.

The day the chickens got loose is a legendary tale from 1963 that has since grown into innumerable versions. It's "The Day of the Chickens" for historical purposes and no one except Captain Bell remembers it as a day of agony.

Nesting in the wingwall, this seagull displays blind faith in BC ferry skippers.

Bell guided *Queen of Victoria* out of Swartz Bay terminal at 7 a.m. smack into one of the most ferocious storms in modern coastal history. It was a gale that closed down all shipping—even tugs—for most of the day and ultimately toppled a massive crane barge at Tsawwassen Terminal. The crane at Tsawwassen was repairing the fire-damaged main dock. Bell's target was the far less sophisticatd auxiliary berth. He tried to inch the big ship into the slot as waves and wind pounded him, but finally he was caught in a surge and found himself crosswise to the dolphins, pinned firmly by winds rushing from the Straits. He radioed for help, but the tug boat fleet was grounded by the storm. The ship remained there all day. "We fought to minimize damage. . . . every crash against the dolphins meant more damage. It was aggravating—I was absolutely powerless against the sea," Bell recalls. "Passengers were terrified at first, but our crew was great, serving free coffee and food to everyone."

Late in the day, down on the car deck, a truckload of live chickens took its place in history. The pounding broke loose about 20 crates of chickens and the little critters ran wild. Captain John Poole, Bell's mate that day, remembers them running through the engine room. "We were picking feathers up everywhere for weeks after," he says. Others saw them on the car decks. There were reports of Chinese cooks jamming them into lunch boxes. Captain Bell says none got off the car deck but it was a hullaballo rounding them up and cleaning the mess of droppings and feathers afterwards.

Monty Aldous has a different recollection. He spent the day powerless and frustrated at head office in Victoria, desperately worried about passengers, crew and his ship. Toward the end of the day, the phone rang. It was *The Vancouver Sun*. The reporter said he had heard that a bunch of chickens had sprung loose and asked Aldous how many.

Aldous says he told the reporter, "I've had a very busy day. . . . I've not yet had time to count them."

It was, in fact, a masterful bit of seamanship by Bell, Poole and the entire crew. When the seas died down and *Queen of Victoria* made it into berth, damage, while expensive to repair, was merely cosmetic. The ship was able to return to Victoria that night with a full load of cars and passengers.

Queen of Burnaby, *identical to* Saanich *(above), went off by herself at Nanaimo.*

There was the day of the runaway ship. Jimmy Bell was up at sunrise one beautiful August morning, in his Nanaimo home overlooking Departure Bay. He was shaving and preparing to take *Queen of Burnaby* out on her 7 a.m. sailing. He glanced out his window enjoying the usually pretty sight of a BC ferry gliding out into the bay. Then he dropped the razor in complete shock, "Good God, there goes the *Queen of Burnaby.*" He shouted to his wife, "Look at your alarm clock!—I've missed the boat!" Soon a phone call informed him that the ship was a runaway.

The night before, someone had left the bridge throttle in the "slow ahead" mode rather than "neutral." An early morning engineer conducted a test on the engine down below and soon sensed to his horror that he was moving. Mooring lines had torn loose from the terminal and the ship leisurely worked her way toward Brandon Island. The quick-thinking engineer stopped the engines, charged to the deck and dropped anchor.

The same thing happened on another day with less humorous results. Captain Bell was ashore at Burrard Drydock when he heard a wailing crunch. His ship had backed into Vancouver Harbor taking a

chunk of the pier with it. Same problem with the bridge control. Same engine room experiment.

Funerals at sea are not encouraged by BC Ferries, but many captains have done them on occasion, usually for the families of deceased colleagues. Bell did them several times, always out of the eyesight of uninvolved passengers. It is merely a memorial service with the sprinkling of the ashes over the sea, but with full formal pomp, prayers, slowing of the ship, lowering the standards and the captain's chant of the "Seaman's Psalm," Psalm 107 beginning with, "Those who go down to the sea in ships. . . ."

SEAMENS' PSALM 107

Some go down to the sea and travel over it in ships, to do business in great waters; these see the works of the Lord, and his wonders in the deep. For He commands and raises the stormy wind, which lifts up the waves of the sea. Those abroad mount up to the heavens, they go down again to the deeps; their courage melts away because of their plight. They reel to and fro, and stagger like a drunken man and are at their wits end—all their wisdom has come to nothing. Then they cry to the Lord in their trouble, and He brings them out of their distresses. He hushes the storm to a calm and gentle whisper, so that the waves of the sea are still. Then the men are glad, because of the calm, and He brings them to their desired haven.

As Bell describes it, "There is real drama. . . .pure Hollywood. Who could get a funeral like that for two bucks?" (The price of a BC Ferry fare at the time.)

On one occasion, Captain Bell, solemnizing the passing of a former chief steward, entertained the man's entire family from Saskatchewan. The service was suitably moving but the wind took the man's ashes in the wrong direction and most of them landed on the ship. The family was still tearfully grateful.

Through the explosive years of ferry growth, all British Columbians were forced to exercise patience. An era of unprecedented shipbuilding and stretching was unable to avert the occasional long waits at terminals.

After the service, Captain Bell and his mate, subsequently a master, Al Heater, were having coffee in the dining room when the deceased's father came over to the table. He asked if he could express his appreciation with a small financial donation. The officers humbly declined and the man retreated. He was back moments later to inquire whether a bottle of spirits would be acceptable. Bell and Heater thought for a moment and then advised that there'd be no harm in that. The dad responded, "Here's ten dollars—go buy a bottle of rum." He ran before it could be refused, but was soon back to fling a five-dollar bill on the table. "And this is for the mix," he said.

James V. Bell Sr. of Vancouver sent his son and namesake Jimmy on a four-year sea apprenticeship in 1935, when the lad was just sixteen. The indenture with a Welsh shipowner began with a wage of 10 pounds sterling annually, rising to 14 pounds by the fourth year. When the war broke out in 1939, Bell was stranded on his ship in Turkey, but he desperately wanted to get home to join the air force. He never made it, but he did reach Britain, where he enlisted in the Royal Air Force. Jimmy Bell was to have a distinguished six-year career, most of it based in Burma, rising to the rank of Warrant Officer by 1945. Gunner, parachute jump master, bombardier, he flew several hundred missions and earned the British *Operation Wing and Bar,* the *King's Badge* and a medal from Chiang Kai-shek.

One noted wartime historical reference mentions Bell and relates a story that still brings tears to his eyes. Two years before the war ended, a friend gave him a Labrador Retriever which he named "Radar." The dog was soon to become base mascot and Bell won permission from his commanding officer to take the pet on flying missions. "The dog was amazing. . . . When we were flying and the flak came at us, he and I would duck for cover at the same time," Bell said.

Radar became knowledgeable about all routines. When Jimmy gathered parachute and flying gear, the dog knew they were off to work. When master spruced up for a night on the town with the boys, Radar knew he was uninvited and he curled up on his bunk.

When the war ended, Bell was based in Karachi, Pakistan, at a Royal Air Force base. He began the process of demobilization, knowing that there was no possible way he could take the dog through post-war red tape and confusion to Vancouver. Bell was certain he could get Radar as far as Calcutta, but that would be the end of the animal. He opted instead to leave his pet at the established base where he would have many friends.

"When I was packed and ready to go, I could tell Radar knew it was for good. He wouldn't stay behind. . . . despite everything I tried, he followed me to the bus. . . . And when the driver insisted we leave to catch the plane, Radar kept chasing after us through a cloud of dust . . . . I could tell what he was thinking. . . . 'You bastard, after all we have been through together,' " Bell related.

After the war, home in Vancouver, Jimmy Bell eventually found himself back at sea. This time, though, he began the academic and apprenticeship programs leading to master's certification. Until his move to BC Ferries in 1960, he served in every available Canadian Pacific ship on the west coast, convinced that his company was buying the wrong kind of vessels for the future market, particularly for the movement of vehicles.

"We couldn't get cars off those ships fast even if we used dynamite," Bell said.

The instant the government announced it was going into the ferry business, Bell wrote to Phil Gaglardi, to offer his services. Gaglardi politely replied that he should wait until jobs were advertised. Bell did, and he became an "original" with BC Ferries. Over the years, many fascinating individuals would work for the company, but, even in that league, Jimmy Bell stands alone.

During the less then formal chat with the author in 1985, Jimmy Bell (right) was asked why so many of BC Ferries best stories centred on him. He replied, "I'm just a character, I guess."

SYSTEMS DEVELOPMENT

Starting out in an organizational sea of pandemonium, BC Ferries took considerable time to establish smoothly operating systems. As many bad ideas as good ones came and went. Humorous stories abound.

There was a valid concern for the security of cash handling in the terminals and on the ships. At the terminal toll booths, someone suggested that security cameras be pinned squarely on the attendant and the cash drawer, not an unusual concept. What was unusual was a decision to let the public do the monitoring. Television sets were placed inside the terminal waiting room and cafeteria and the public sat transfixed, staring at hands changing cash. Unfortunately, if a cashier happened to drop a coin and stooped out of camera range, the spectators would rise in an uproar, convinced that grand larceny was taking place and pointing accusing fingers. Fish bowl security didn't last long.

At first BC Ferries didn't worry too much about defining the term "hand luggage" for foot passengers, until the company learned how broadly the term could be interpreted. One chap showed up one day with twenty concrete lawn ornaments. Another guy had fifty suitcases with him. One lady had with her an animal in a huge cage, towing it on a hand trolley. An attendant lifted the curtain on the cage expecting to see a dog, and reeled in horror at the sight of a live leopard. On the northern service, native Indians from Bella Bella regularly arrived towing their worldly possessions, expecting to pay only the passenger fare. The company finally instituted a rule defining "hand luggage" as being up to 66 pounds, but it continues to be loosely enforced.

Animal stories are plentiful. An immigrant couple showed up at Swartz Bay one day with an old horse on the back of a dilapidated truck. They were heading to the Gulf Islands to clear a piece of property, but they didn't have enough money for the fare. Swartz Bay terminal agent Denny Keen remembers, "He rushed over to his wife and tried to pull her ring off her finger. It was to be security for credit." Keen took pity on him. The chap, his wife and the horse boarded the small island ferry, but the old truck sat at the terminal for two months. Another fellow enquired how much the fare would be to transport a horse and rider. Keen called Assistant General Manager Ron Worley who instructed, "Don't charge him anything, as long as he brings a broom and a shovel to clean up the mess." The chap followed instructions.

A less happy event occurred for a passenger at Swartz Bay. A customer in a fancy new convertible car arrived early one day for the ferry, parking in a lane next to a large cattle truck. The driver left the car and walked over to the cafeteria. By the time he returned, the roof of his car was splattered black with cow manure which had somehow worked its way through the slats of the cattle truck. The car roof was ruined and BC Ferries paid for repairs.

During the course of one sailing from the islands, a prize bull escaped its confinement and jumped overboard, prompting a reversal of the vessel and a heroic rescue. The bull paddled around until ropes could secure it. The whole crew and the animal's owner played a mighty tug of war before the bull was hoisted back onto the car deck.

Then there was the hijacker, armed with several beehives. A lady and her husband drove up to Tsawwassen before sailing time. The woman stayed with the bees while he went into the cafeteria. He said he would walk aboard the ferry and meet her there. Unfortunately, she got into the wrong line and the wrong ship. As her husband sailed for the Gulf Islands, she was en-route to Victoria. The lady asked the chief steward if the ferry could make an emergency stop on the island. Word came back from the captain that this would be impossible. When the woman said she had a truck full of bees on the car deck and would let them loose on the ship, a hasty policy change brought the vessel into Mayne Island.

One time a farmer walked up to a small islands vessel with a live goat in tow. The mate at the time and subsequently a major vessels master, Bob Andersen, was collecting the fare. The farmer asked how much to transport the goat. Andersen mused for a moment or two and then wrote in his book, "One kid, one dollar."

During the mid-1960s BC Ferries inadvertently found itself in the middle of a titanic struggle between W.A.C. Bennett and Canadian Pacific Investments. The ferry company innocently was looking for office space to house the ever-growing passenger information services. They thought they had made an ideal arrangement within the Empress Hotel complex. Smoke clouds soon billowed from the premier's office and the lease was vetoed.

Just prior to that, Premier Bennett learned that CP, never his favorite company, had retained a New York consultant to prepare a report justifying tearing down the Empress. The historic institution was in dreadful shape at the time. The buildings still operated on British-style direct current. Guests had to use adaptors for their electric razors. Televisions wouldn't function on the system. Canadian Pacific faced a crossroads—either pump millions into the old edifice or replace her with a modern tower. Nevertheless, the British Columbia premier dispatched an edict to Montreal. Canadian Pacific was told in blunt terms that if they so much as removed a brick from the Empress, the company would never again do a penny of business in British Columbia. The railway giant went into full reverse and finally started pumping a huge modernization investment into their celebrated Victoria property. A budding CP executive at the time and now general manager of the Empress, Ted Balderson says that Bennett's intervention at the time was "very influential."

Queen of the Islands' innaugural party at Ganges in 1963 became a series of misadventures. The locals dressed in finery and costumes, when the ship broke down in the Straits, were forced to wait too long. An overabundance of refreshments produced predictable results.

LAUNCH MISFIRES

The frequent christening of new BC Ferries ships, in the early 1960s, were usually grand events. Various dignitaries would be assigned to crash the champagne and the crowd would enjoy various refreshments. However, some of these launches didn't go exactly as planned.

Queen of the Islands has been perhaps the least loved of any new ship ever to serve in the system. She had excellent passenger amenities, with panoramic 360-degree exposure to scenery, but that's where the joy ended. Her engines produced nothing but difficulty, the car deck was a jigsaw puzzle to load, and unless loading was done with meticulous precision, she sailed with a pronounced list. Her years of upcoming difficulty might have been forecast at her official commencement in 1963.

W.A.C. Bennett, who had a summer place on Salt Spring, ordered a party to celebrate the island's first link to the mainland by BC Ferries. Bob Innes, longtime marketing and public relations executive, remembers well that great occasion in Ganges on Salt Spring Island. "It was a situation you had to be in to believe it."

Innes and an associate arrived early and first reported to the home of the famous island's ferry skipper, Captain George Maude, who had founded the Gulf Islands Ferry Service in 1930 and remained in charge until the BC Ferries takeover. "Just as we approached the front door, this ferocious roar came from nowhere," Innes recalls. After ducking for cover, he discovered that Captain Maude's son had an airplane mounted in the back yard—no wings, but a noisy engine. "It was a bad omen," Innes says.

As the premier, his guests, the Gulf Islands notables and hundreds of Salt Spring children—dressed for the event as little Indians and pirates—sat waiting for the arrival of the new ship, word came that *Queen of the Islands* had broken down in the middle of the Straits. Tug boats had been called. She would be late and likely under tow. The pirates and Indians became restless and the dignitaries squirmed in the heat.

Bob Innes had another problem. He had arranged for special corsages for the ladies on the reviewing stand. They were to come from a florist shop in Duncan. They hadn't arrived, but, just as the ship, towed by tugs, swung into view, Innes recalls, "The flowers roll

Queen of Prince Rupert's *1966 maiden voyage to her northern namesake, was triumphant. The fishing fleet swarmed around her.*

up in a bloody hearse!...I couldn't even find a warehouse to hide it behind."

As he was attending to the VIP ladies with the corsages, a group of 40-year-old women who had been partying all day, "were just a winging when they came across the dock." But what Bob Innes remembers as "le piece de resistance," occurred sometime later. As soon as the speeches were over, the audience scrambled aboard *Queen of the Islands* and gobbled up all the food.

"There wasn't even a donut left for the premier and the VIPs.... We got them out of there rather quickly," Innes says.

Queen of Prince Rupert has been an important ship in the fleet since her launch in 1966. With her passenger staterooms and amenities, a live-aboard crew, and the long, beautiful route though the Inside Passage, she instantly became W.A.C. Bennett's favorite and the flagship. Her respective masters and crews also knew for years that they were something special and never hesitated to lord it over their colleagues on the more basic southern transportation routes.

When any BC Ferry ship approaches a terminal, the captain radios ahead the impending arrival stating the name of the vessel and the terminal tower acknowledges. In her glory days, *Queen of Prince Rupert* would radio her arrival, *"The Queen* approaching Tsawwassen Terminal," and the shore operator, for whom "Queens" were as commonplace as fishing boats, would wearily shout back, "Queen Who?" When accused of arrogance, *The Rupert's* captains would describe it as habit. In the home ports of Prince Rupert and Kelsey Bay, there was only one Queen.

Queen of Prince Rupert's official launch in October 1965 proved to be the harbinger of a fascinating career. Premier Bennett had eagerly awaited this $6 million semi-cruise ship to extend the long hand of BC Ferries to northerly Prince Rupert. As a large crowd of dignitaries looked on awaiting the wife of Legislature Speaker W.H. Murray to crash the champagne bottle against *Queen of Prince Rupert's* bow, a youngster ran past, tripping the wire that triggered the ship's release down the slip. *QPR* started moving toward the water and Mrs. Murray stood in shock. Urged by a shipyard official

to fling the champagne bottle hung on a long string, she hurled the bubbly but the bottle harmlessly bounced off as the gleaming new vessel gaily started backing across the harbor. Only the quick action of nearby tugs prevented it from demolishing a government wharf. The champagne finally was broken against her hull at the pier. There was little cause for hurry. The master scheduled to take her north had been suddenly hospitalized for minor surgery, forcing a one-month sailing delay.

An accident to *Queen of Prince Rupert* a year later indirectly contributed to the Seattle-based service of Alaska State Ferries. Naval architect Phillip F. Spaulding of Seattle, who has done work for all the ferry services in the Pacific Northwest says that Alaska only wanted to come as far south as Prince Rupert, connecting with both the British Columbia highways system and the ferry service. Alaska State Ferry customers complained frequently about the highways conditions between Prince George and Prince Rupert—construction was proceeding slowly at the time. But the State Ferry system remained patient, referring people to *Queen of Prince Rupert*. Everyone was happy until the British Columbia ship ran aground and was out of commission for several months. It was at this point, according to Spaulding, that Alaska decided to make its bold thrust south to Seattle.

BC Ferries, however, has enjoyed a long history of co-operation with the ships of Alaska. Up until the start of British Columbia's Queen Charlotte Islands service in 1981, the two companies shared the same berth in Prince Rupert. Joint information services and interline ticketing developed and, where possible, schedules have been adjusted to conveniently transfer passengers from one fleet to the other. Mutual co-operation continues.

THE GANG THAT COULDN'T SHOOT STRAIGHT

One night in December 1971, Saltery Bay ticket agent, Allen Reavie, had some strange visitors. While counting his cash at closing time, he responded to a tapping at the door. Two masked men shoved themselves into the booth, nervously shaking guns in their hands. "I feared one of us might be shot from the vibrations alone," Reavie said.

One of the men went to empty the safe and cash drawer, while the other faced a serious engineering problem. A little guy about 5'2", barely able to see through inadequate eye holes in the head bag that kept moving around, he was attempting to bind up the 6'4" Reavie within the confined space. After several contortionist maneuvers, nearly strangling Reavie in the process, the robber realized he hadn't brought enough rope for so large a victim. The ticket agent helped by bending down. Reavie, once roughly bound, was told to kneel. The agent pointed out there was no way for him to do this short of toppling over like a bowling pin. The intruders assisted him to the floor.

The robbers discussed gagging their victim, but discovered they didn't have anything with them that would do the job. They asked Reavie, but he was short of gagging supplies as well. Then they asked where the phone was, and ripped it out of the wall. The office lights were the next concern and after being told where the switch was, the place went into abject blackness. It was too dark for them to find their way out. On went the lights and one of the thieves ran to the car to turn on the headlights.

This accomplished, he returned to report that his gun was missing. Reavie had to roll over on the floor to prove that he wasn't hiding it. They decided the weapon must be in the car. They asked the agent where his car keys were, and he replied that they were in the ignition of the vehicle parked outside. Out went the lights again, and the crooks started their getaway. But they stopped to argue in the parking lot about which car to take, the ticket agent's or the little one they stole in Powell River. After deciding it would be unprofessional to leave the "hot" car at the crime scene, they drove off in both.

Allen Reavie quickly untied himself and walked 50 feet up the road to a pay phone. He called the RCMP. Five miles down the road, the robbers ditched the "hot" car and proceeded in Reavie's vehicle straight into a police roadblock. When they tried to ram their way through, the car careened madly into a ditch. A jail term followed.

BC Ferry terminal superintendant Gerry Barber had a more sophisticated visitor during his Black Ball days at Horseshoe Bay. He and an assistant were crammed into a tiny toll booth. The assistant bent over to retrieve something just as a gun-toting bandit pulled up in a car. When he heard the threatening demand for all the money, the assistant happily stayed pinned to the floor. Barber handed over the cash and the crook ordered him to lie down on the floor. Barber did his best, squashing his partner in the process. It was not good enough for this "Al Capone." Menacingly, he waved the gun and Barber crushed his breathless mate. The thief sped away, soon to be apprehended in a road block.

Captain John Smith had a hair-raising experience one day on the Horseshoe Bay-Nanaimo crossing. A psychiatric case rushed the bridge with a .22 rifle. A quartermaster, who saw the guy, ran to the ship's chief engineer. They debated what to do as the captain was held hostage. A plan unfolded that the engineer would sneak up behind the villain with a heavy spanner. Others warned him, "Don't do that, he might shoot the old man!" Thankfully, Captain Smith was able to talk the intruder out of it and police were waiting on the other side. They never did figure out what he wanted.

One incident was potentially serious. At the height of British Columbia's Dukhobor uprising, a bomb went off in a pile of life jackets. No one was aboard at the time and damage was minimal.

A guard transporting a prisoner to William Head Prison near Victoria lost his charge on a ship one day. The guard thought his prisoner was harmless, and let him go off to the washroom by himself. When he failed to return, the corrections officer, now apoplectic, raced from one end of the ship to the other failing to find his ward. He reported the matter to the chief steward who suggested they try to have the guy paged. The guard rolled his eyes toward heaven, but the chief said it wouldn't hurt to try. "Would Mr. John Doe please report to the magazine stand," the steward announced throughout the ship. Sure enough, John Doe arrived, completely surprised that anyone was worried. "I was sitting over there with a bunch of girls," he told the near-homicidal guard.

TIME MAGAZINE—THE HARD WAY

On a pleasant summer day in 1972, Captain James V. Bell, aboard Queen of Burnaby, *approached the routine fail-safe, point-of-no-return into what the masters euphemistically call* Cardiac Cove—Horseshoe Bay. *Once a major ship rounds the final blind turn, there is nothing left to do but go straight into the berth—no time for the slightest bit of maneuvering. The alternatives are to argue with a sheer cliff or to make significant renovations to Sewell's Marina.*

As the tiny bay unfolded before him, Bell spotted the usual array of pleasure boats, most of which had the good sense to scamper away in response to the blast of the ship's horn. One tiny boat refused to budge. Later testimony would show that a macho young man in the boat calmly told his girlfriend passenger that the ship would go around. Anxiously, Captain Bell did what little he could as he went into the berth, and the tiny boat made a futile, desperate attempt to get out of the way. It was a grazing miss, the boat capsized, and the young couple went for a swim.

Bell sighed with relief and dispatched his mate and deck officers to supervise the unloading and loading of vehicles. Moments later, a huge athletic apparition, dripping wet, loomed on the bridge where the captain was alone. Somehow, in his rage, the boater had bypassed everyone. Bell was pounded squarely on the nose, knocked to the deck, and a scuffle ensued. The captain soon managed to scramble away. He rushed to the bridge wing, jumped a chain guarding the bridge exterior entrance, went down a ladder and eventually found colleagues to help. The boater was apprehended and ultimately convicted of assault, adding one more chapter in the War of Horseshoe Bay.

The bruised Captain Bell was perplexed by the odd press story that sympathized with the young brute. He was much mollified a few days later when he became only the second employee in BC Ferries history to make Time Magazine. *W.A.C. Bennett was the other. "I made* Time *the hard way," he says.*

Small craft owners frequently display appalling ignorance about seamanship, a daily headache for large vessel masters.

SOLID LANDINGS
CHAPTER SEVEN

"When your bridge wing is covered with splinters and your ship is in lane three of the parking lot, you know it's not going to be a dull day."—an anonymous captain.

Few captains in a long career at sea have not had an "incident"— sticking a ship on a reef, having a fire, a grounding, rescue, medical emergency or mechanical failure. These range from the humorous to the tragic. A typical BC Ferries skipper will make between 1,500 and 2,000 landings each year in all weather conditions. Berthing creates most of the mishaps.

In the 25-year history there have been hundreds of unfortunate events, most involving little more than a dent and terminal damage. A moment of inattention by the captain or mate is usually the cause. Sometimes it's another vessel. A shipping curiosity seems to be that the worst accidents often occur under the command of the most admired masters, the theory being that the best may tend to be more nonchalant and prone to boredom, while the less competent are more wary and more "by-the-book." The number one enemy is not training, licensing, qualifications, equipment or human ability, but the simple monotony of scheduled shuttle service. In BC Ferries annals, recorded incidents have led to suspensions, demotions, dismissals and various court actions against officers. Negligence has occurred and has not been tolerated. But the extenuating circumstances are usually so pronounced that every sympathy rests with the officers involved.

Although by June 15, 1985, BC Ferries had carried 187,000,000 people safely to their destinations, three passenger deaths occurred in an incident where another ship was held predominantly to blame. The company has witnessed the occasional suicide and deaths from medical causes. A welder was killed in a fire at Tsawwassen and an engineer was once crushed to death by a watertight door in a northern ship, and, on one occasion, a ship painter fell to his death. A tragedy involving *Queen of Cowichan,* between Bowen Island and West Vancouver, occurred in August, 1985. Three people on a small pleasure craft died after a collision with the ship. The investigation into the incident is continuing.

Some ships live a life of charm, eccentricity and sometimes unfortunate events. Within BC Ferries, Queen of Prince Rupert *trails only* Queen of Victoria *in the assembly of anecdotal tales. During the summer of 1980, replaced on the northern run by the more lavish* Queen of the North, QPR *was sent south to replace the popular and historic* Princess Marquerite *(opposite page, bottom) on the Victoria to Seattle dayliner service. Gaily painted as* Victoria Princess, Queen of Prince Rupert *is shown (top and immediate left). The experiment was short-lived.* The Maggie, *and* QPR *returned to normal service the next year.*

Accidents make such spectacular film footage and news stories that these clippings dominate newspaper records. Historical shipping memories based on these files are a gross distortion of reality. Modern shipping is the safest form of transport mankind has ever known. Horses, buses, railways, aircraft and the menacing automobile deserve far more attention from those seeking dramatic tragedy.

Safety drills, fire inspections, formal certification, lifeboat practice, evacuation exercises and regular inspections by government and industry agencies are a routine part of life on BC Ferry ships. They combine to form an unparalleled safety record, of which the company is justly proud.

However, despite this record, from the earliest days, W.A.C. Bennett was never amused to see pictures of ships in embarrassing situations. He was aboard a ferry one time when he saw a little book about the company on the newsstand. Leafing through it, he found a photo of *M.V. Chinook II* aground on Snake Island. The premier immediately ordered the book removed from the entire fleet.

Many of the incidents have also produced humorous anecdotes. Employees remember an early master who had a propensity for knocking over dolphins and wingwalls. He became known as "Captain Crunch."

THERE GO I BUT FOR THE GRACE OF GOD....

The late Captain Brian Biddick, a senior master with the Peninsular & Oriental Steam Navigation Company, was home on leave one time when he got a call from head office. He was informed that a colleague had put *Pacific Princess*—The Love Boat—on a Mexican reef. Biddick was asked to head the company's enquiry into the affair. Biddick advised the executive that the captain in question was his best friend and that it would be inadvisable for him to participate. P&O insisted. "We are sure you will be very professional, Brian." On this occasion, thankfully, the fault rested with a Mexican

pilot, but, as Biddick said at a later date, "A ship accident is truly the business of 'there go I but for the grace of God.' "

For the curious, newspaper files will give the names of BC Ferries officers involved in serious incidents and the repercussions that followed. All suffered embarrassment and some never truly recovered either professionally or personally. No purpose will be served by raking it up again on these pages. However, the story of one master may help shed some insight on the chemistry of major events. A captain was commended for extraordinary seamanship in the face of one emergency, but found himself under the glare of possible censure in another.

Queen of Victoria was proceeding at 22 knots through Active Pass in 1976, pushed by strong winds and tidal action, when a fire erupted in the engine room. Captain Al Bahry lost all power as the ship charged toward Laura Bluff on Galiano Island. In a brilliant emergency maneuver, he ordered both anchors dropped from the bow and the ship's momentum forced a complete reversal of direction. Only truly heroic efforts by the engineers to douse the flames with carbon dioxide, prevented tragedy. "We almost lost three men in the engine room. . . .The ship was out of service for a month," Captain Bahry said.

The unhappy circumstance was in August 1979, when he took command of *Queen of Alberni* for the first time, a far different ship from the traditional vessels of BC Ferries. The "double enders" have wheelhouses and a single giant propeller at each end of the ship. They never have to turn 180 degrees. But a more important difference in this instance was that the jumbo "double enders" have a deep V-shaped hull configuration, unlike the shallow and flatter bottoms he was used to on the rest of the fleet. The 7 a.m. sailing on August 9 was Bahry's first crossing of Active Pass in this new class of ship. Midway through the pass, he heard the terrifying crunch of Collinson Reef against the hull of his ship.

In the wake of the event, Captain Bahry sat stoically through various hearings, taking full responsibility and sharing none of the blame with his subordinate officers, or other traffic that happened to be in the pass at the time. He said little on his own behalf, but the company entered evidence that Bahry had previously commanded

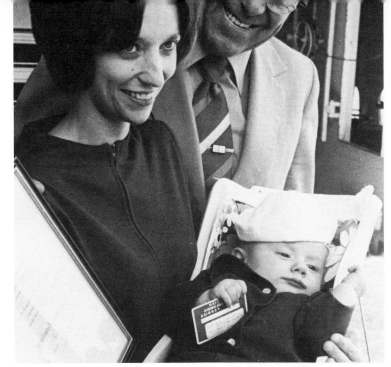

8,000 successful and safe trips through Active Pass. The tribunal ruled that Bahry had committed "an error of judgment" (the mildest form of rebuke) and he was quickly reinstated by BC Ferries to full command.

A native of Vegreville, Alberta, Al Bahry went to sea as a young lad. He had some deep sea experience in the ships of Shell and Imperial Oil, before a long career up and down the west coast with Canadian Pacific and Northland Navigation. He served as chief officer aboard *Smokwa* and *Bainbridge* before Black Ball was taken over by BC Ferries. His first command was *Queen of Sidney* in 1970. Throughout his days with the company, and to the present, Al Bahry has been one of the best liked and most admired masters in the system.

Years after the *Queen of Alberni* incident, he said privately that his memories are "full of maybes" and that he still doesn't know what he might have done differently. He was fully aware of the reef, the draught of the ship, the BC Ferry coming the other way and the many fishing boats in his path. "My intent was to miss everything."

After the chilling scrape and the certain knowledge of grounding, Bahry said, "At that point, to all intents and purposes, I think that's it. . . .I've lost my job. And you set about getting everybody off safely." But he said the crew—from galley staff and the cafeteria ladies to the seamen—performed with cool aplomb. "They surpass your expectations." He had equal praise for the calmness of the passengers. "They know you are in a tough spot and you will get them out of it." (There was considerable vehicle and ship damage in the incident and the death of one horse, but there were no passenger injuries.)

During the growth years, BC Ferries were always quick to seize promotional opportunities. In the top photo, a lifetime pass is presented to the first baby born on a company ship: Gordon Wayne "Skipper" Earwaker. The birth occurred May 3, 1971 aboard Queen of Victoria.

103

The private torment for the captain began back at home. "You dare not answer your phone. . . . You know it's likely just some well-meaning friends. . .but you can't afford to say anything. . . .Some of it could get out before the hearings are held, or to the press," he said. Captain Bahry quoted a fellow master who had suffered a similar circumstance. "You feel a great sense of loneliness."

MISHAP MADNESS

American mobster Lucky Luciano once said, "There's a little larceny in everyone." It's a comment that carries much meaning for the BC Ferry personnel asked to adjudicate public claims in the wake of a mishap. Most of the passengers are reasonable and the company is both generous and apologetic, but always a number of people try to take advantage of the situation.

The *Queen of Alberni* accident created the greatest havoc. With the ship perched heavily on the reef, the list grew even more pronounced with the failing tide, to the point where it was feared that she might roll over. However, she remained secure in the ungainly position, but the vehicles on the car deck piled on top of one another.

Tsawwassen terminal agent Gerry Barber looked after the evacuated passengers who glumly awaited their vehicles. "We towed cars off that ship that were not much bigger than garbage cans," he recalled. Passengers were dispatched in taxis at BC Ferries' expense to hotels, the airport or wherever they wanted to go. An employee was dispatched to a drug store to bring back a carload of toiletries, shaving gear and disposable diapers as many passengers made the Tsawwassen terminal their home for the day. The cafeteria churned out a steady flow of free food.

"One guy claimed for a car we couldn't find," Barber remembers. "We finally discovered that he never even had a car."

But the best tale came from the owner of the horse that died aboard *Queen of Alberni,* coincidentally a BC Ferries employee. The owner put in a claim of $30,000 for the racehorse, *Gun Music.* Fortunately, someone in the company remembered that the horse had been purchased two weeks earlier in a claiming race for $2,500.

They settled for $3,200. The employee also filed for "bereavement leave" under the terms of the union contract. This too was denied.

Engineering supervisor (south) A.C. "Sandy" Ritchie's favorite traveling companions are a 1971 white Lincoln Continental and a perpetual black cloud. He and his trusty car were aboard *Queen of Alberni* when she went aground in Active Pass. As the ship perched precariously on the reef, Ritchie was relieved to see that his car had survived intact. When the ship was righted, he watched, with a sense of horror and helplessness, as a large tractor trailer rolled on top of his vehicle. "The Lincoln was reduced in height by eight inches," he said. The accident gave Ritchie a sense of deja vu. He had been aboard *Chinook II* when she ran aground on Snake Island in 1962. That time, sea water rose up to the hubcaps of his Ford Fairlane.

With the foolishness displayed by some members of the public, it is amazing that there have not been more serious accidents. One day *Langdale Queen* was in the final stages of loading at Horseshoe Bay. The mate was about to give the "all clear" to the master up on the bridge when he thought he heard a noise under the car deck aft. A man and his family were underneath in small boat staring in fascination at the ship's glimmering propeller, churning slowly in the idle position. "You would have seen arms and legs and pieces of boat going by you," a witness recalled.

One of the more amusing accidents, except for those involved and the company, occurred at Vesuvius Bay on Salt Spring Island. As the vessel approached her berth, the engineer left an oiler alone in the engine room. Just prior to berthing, the oiler walked into a pipe and knocked himself cold. When the captain telegraphed the "slow ahead" command, there was no one to carry out the instruction. By the time the bridge reacted to the failed response, it was too late. *Vesuvius Queen* hurtled into the dock at 9 knots, damaging the terminal, several cars aboard and the vessel. The company refused to accept the engineer's excuse that he was using the toilet at the time and there were reprimands.

A seaman's greatest terror is fire and the most stringent safety measures of the company deal with its prevention and suppression. Crews are regularly trained in firefighting.

Captain Peter de Cunha, a shore-based company executive for the past twenty years, remembers a day at sea when a real explosion occurred aboard a ship, unbeknownst to the passengers aboard. Later examination discovered that a bent pipe on the ship's funnel was dripping oil down onto a hot manifold. There was a distinct "boom" and the beginning of a fire, but it was brought under control in minutes. When passengers saw the smoke, the chief steward announced over the public address system, "I'm sorry ladies and gentlemen but the air conditioning is out of order." De Cunha remembers, as perilously close as the incident was to a real calamity, "We didn't even miss a trip."

De Cunha was in command of *Queen of Victoria* on November 13, 1962, when fire at Tsawwassen Terminal produced one of the company's rare tragedies. As he approached the berth, de Cunha could see smoke billowing from the main terminal. The control tower told him that the fire was well clear of the auxiliary berth. The captain ordered out the fire hoses and had his crew turn them on full force, creating a wall of water between his ship and the fire. "The water didn't even reach the fire," de Cunha recalls. It was determined that a welder's spark ignited the blaze. The welder's body was not discovered until a month later when it washed up on the Tsawwassen causeway.

De Cunha figured in a more frivolous event a couple of years prior. One day, as a chief officer, he was supervising the unloading of cars at Tsawwassen, standing erect in his best British military bearing. The last vehicle off the ship carried a huge German Shepherd hanging out the passenger window. The officer's gold braid was too much for the dog. As the truck went by, the dog snapped, neatly ripping the entire sleeve off at the shoulder. In shock, de Cunha looked up the parking lot to see the truck disappearing and his sleeve hanging from the dog's mouth.

Swartz Bay Terminal suffered a fire in December 1981. A contractor's cutting torch ignited a blaze which was to cause $500,000 damage, destroying a wingwall and a substantial portion of the passenger walkway. Within minutes of its eruption, the terminal crew, some trained in fire fighting, were able to hold back the blaze. *Queen of Nanaimo,* approaching berth at the time, brought her hoses to bear. Within eight minutes, Saanich fire trucks were on the scene. There were no injuries.

All areas of the ship, particularly the danger zones of the engine room and the galleys, are equipped with carbon dioxide fire extinguishing equipment. One day, a galley hand accidentally tripped the automatic carbon dioxide lever and pandemonium erupted. The crew fled the galley in full panic as a good many dinners were blanketed in white foam.

No one at BC Ferries has ever been able to fully explain why a preponderance of the company's worst accidents have occurred during the month of August. Pleasure craft are plentiful and sometimes hazardous. Often there can be morning fog, but the weather tends to be the best of the year.

THE PRETENDER

If *Queen of Victoria* has any challenger to the throne of mysticism, it can only be *Queen of Prince Rupert.* Her Haddington Reef and Gunboat Passage groundings have passed into company legend but, like *The Vic,* her mystery is not so much because of the serious happenings, but because of an endless series of unusual experiences.

Queen of Prince Rupert has had her scraps with coastal Indians. She was picketed when she arrived to remove industrial equipment from the closed pulp mill at Ocean Falls. Her windows have been caved in by monstrous seas in Hecate Strait and she had an ugly hole carved into her side for an aircraft-style gangway to serve the wooden wharf at Bella Bella. She's crashed into piers and performed more serious search and rescue work than any civilian vessel in British Columbia.

But perhaps her most inglorious summer was that of 1980, when the government accepted a questionable consultant's report about the health of the funky, historic *Princess Marguerite,* and pulled her off the triumphantly successful Seattle-Victoria dayliner run. To appease angry Victoria merchants, who believed reports that *The Maggie* was perfectly safe, the government announced that her replacement would be a combination of the Boeing jetfoil and the *Queen of Prince Rupert.*

BC Ferries had previously rejected the jetfoil, after exhaustive tests under Captain Gus McLeod, as unsuitable and uneconomic for our waters. Outside shipping buffs were dismayed to see *QPR* gaudily painted in Union Jack colors and with a new hole smashed in her exterior to permit side loading. She was too slow, too small, and with much of her tonnage consisting of excessive vehicle capacity and staterooms, totally unsuitable for the Seattle run. But she sailed for a season as *Victoria Princess.* A year later, *Princess Marguerite* regained ovations in the south, and *Her Majesty,* back in the pastel blue of the Dogwood fleet, was similarly acclaimed up north.

THE PSYCHIC SIDE OF SHIPPING

Learned scientists will happily tell you that it is impossible for a collection of nuts, bolts, steel, electronics and upholstery to have an independent personality. Inanimate objects cannot behave in human ways.

Self-evident suppositions like these will be greeted by seamen throughout the world with a knowing wink. Shipping executives shudder about scaring passengers with the word jinx, *but every fleet has at least one ship which has a predilection for, if not disaster, then most certainly the bizarre.*

These scientists have not met Queen of Victoria, *the only real lady of the BC Ferries fleet (despite the use of the name "Queen," the rest of the ships carry masculine names.) In the spring of 1985, when radio newscasts reported that a little girl had fallen off a BC Ferries ship en route to Swartz Bay, company employees would most likely assume, "Must be* The Vic." *It usually is. It was. Six-year-old Fawn Brown of the Gulf Islands owes her life to the nimble and dramatic 180-degree high-speed turn by Captain Bob Andersen, and an adept rescue by crew. The times when the company's millionth car arrived in the 1960s, or when the first of many babies was born on the ships or when a chap drove his car off the stern committing suicide, could have happened on any ship in the fleet. They didn't.*

It was also unfortunate in August 1970, when the Russian freighter Sergey Yesenin—*improperly in Active Pass—rushed out of the fog and sliced into the side of* Queen of Victoria. *There have been many more less serious accidents in the ship's lifetime—perhaps as many as the rest of the fleet combined—but her claim to special status is more for the continuing series of truly offbeat events: rescues of abandoned boaters or drunks who fall overboard and weird passenger behavior. It defies logic.* Queen of Victoria *and* Queen of Vancouver—The Vic *and* The Van—*were launched within three weeks of each other in 1961. Aside from the worst engines the company ever bought (Paxman Twins), which plagued both vessels until replaced in 1981, the* Queen of Vancouver, *identical in every way, has had a positively dull life compared to her sister.*

Despite her colorful career, The Vic *has carried more than her share of the company's passenger millions safely to and from Vancouver Island. Her crews never fail to cheerfully board her, convinced that the chances of a boring day are rather remote.*

Captain John Horn was once asked how two identical sisters, Queen of Victoria *and* Queen of Vancouver, *could handle so differently. Horn replied, "Have you ever made love to identical twins?"*

In this case, Queen of Prince Rupert *was doing the rescuing. Cars drove off the beached Alaska State Ferry* Taku *aboard the British Columbia ship, near Prince Rupert.*

M.V. CHINOOK II— SNAKE ISLAND, APRIL 5, 1962

A dispute between BC Ferries and a supplier over the purchase of radar equipment contributed to the grounding of Chinook II. Black Ball Ferries had leased the equipment but the government thought it was included with the fleet purchase and refused to make payments. One night, the owners arrived and physically removed the devices.

Chinook had a routine crossing of the Strait heading toward Nanaimo, but fog closed in as the ship neared its destination. The captain was blind without radar and tried to navigate by reckoning. The ship thumped upon Snake Island, and, as the tide fell, she was perched precariously, high and dry.

Coincidentally, federal inspectors were aboard examining some fifty BC Ferries employees about evacuation procedures. They were to have a real lesson. Passengers were removed through the stern car doors, and transferred ashore. The crew waited anxiously until a high tide permitted the ship to safely back off the rock and return to duty. Damage was minor.

at Expo

inside

wrong . . .

Why not go to church on Sunday?

THE PROVINCE

15 CENTS

VANCOUVER, B.C., SATURDAY, AUGUST 12, 1967

Shipwreck becomes holiday frolic

By NORMAN HACKING
Province Marine Editor

QUEEN OF PRINCE RUPERT

Hospital agreement reached

Meteors to glow tonight

Teenager trapped in well

...rafts bunched from stricken ferry dot the reef as local fishboats and pleasure craft go in to take passengers ashore to Alert Bay. More pictures on Page 5.

QUEEN OF PRINCE RUPERT—

HADDINGTON REEF, AUGUST 11, 1967

After Queen of Prince Rupert *went aground on Haddington Reef near Alert Bay, the* Vancouver Province *headlined, "SHIPWRECK BECOMES HOLIDAY FROLIC." It was perhaps the most memorable day in the life of the tiny community. At 6 a.m., an officer misread radar information and they beached on the reef. About three hundred passengers were evacuated and taken ashore to Alert Bay. The town opened its hearts and its homes to their surprise guests. BC Ferries bought hot dogs and helped passengers with other travel arrangements. Pool parties spontaneously erupted throughout the town. Native Indians provided the warmest reception of all.*

Despite the inconvenience, the company received numerous letters from passengers for months saying that the adventure was a highlight of their lives. Passengers retrieved their vehicles two days later at Nanaimo. One lady calmly told officials that she had a trunk load of fresh salmon in her car. After two days on the hot car deck, it was not difficult to find the vehicle.

The crew slept aboard the ship until salvage crews could tow her off the reef. The captain finally reported to assistant traffic manager, Dave Price, in Nanaimo that they were moving and would arrive in Nanaimo about four or five in the morning. Price was asked to have some breakfast available for thirty or so crew members so he arranged details with a Chinese cook from a local hotel. Soon after, however, the ship radioed that it was taking on water and would likely have to beach. Price canceled breakfast. Then Queen of Prince Rupert *called again to report that the problem was solved and breakfast was back on again.*

The frustrated, sleepless Chinese cook had the last word on this incident. He told Price, "You people don't know what you are doing. That's the reason the ship went on the rocks in the first place." The incident cost the company $750,000.

Judged to be Canada's top news photograph of 1970, this dramatic shot was taken by then Vancouver Province *photographer Gordon Croucher.*

QUEEN OF VICTORIA— ## ACTIVE PASS, AUGUST 2, 1970

The most memorable crash and the only passenger fatalities in an incident occurred when the Soviet freighter Sergey Yesenin *loomed from nowhere in Active Pass and sliced into the side of* Queen of Victoria. *Three passengers were killed and damage amounted to just under $1 million. Damage to the Russian ship was minor. Major inquiries established that the Canadian pilot on the freighter was mostly to blame, but also faulted the BC Ferry master for not being sufficiently far to starboard. The Soviet Union sent BC Ferries a cheque for $550,000, covering 60 percent of the repairs and lost business revenues. The Russian ship should not have been in Active Pass.*

QUEEN OF ALBERNI—
ACTIVE PASS, AUGUST 9, 1979

When Queen of Alberni, *a jumbo "C" class vessel with a sharp V-shaped hull, hit the reef in Active Pass, it made possible the dramatic photography that haunts captains. There was heavy traffic in the pass and another BC Ferry coming from the other direction. The captain steered too far to starboard and heard the terrifying crunch of the reef. High on the rocks, the ship tipped dangerously to one side and threatened to roll over.*

Cars and trucks crashed together on the car decks causing considerable damage. The only fatality was a racehorse named "Gun Music" worth an estimated $3,200. Passengers were safely evacuated. Damage totalled $1 million.

The company's most expensive incident occurred in drydock, and not at sea.

QUEEN OF PRINCE RUPERT— GUNBOAT PASSAGE, AUGUST 25, 1982

Queen of Prince Rupert *was behind schedule in her run south to Port Hardy and the captain decided to take a shortcut through Gunboat Passage near Bella Bella. Although not the recommended route, the pass is navigable, but the master inexplicably steered to the wrong side of a marker buoy and grounded the ship.*

After being pulled from the reef, the ship made its own way back to Bella Bella, where the 300 passengers were transferred to Queen of the North. *Those with cars waited overnight at Port Hardy to be reunited with their 59 vehicles.* Queen of Prince Rupert *made it south to Port Hardy, arriving ten hours after her big sister.*

BC Ferries picked up all the costs and some elements of mardi gras enjoyed fifteen years earlier at Alert Bay recurred. Damage was $500,000. Some passengers were properly angered by the incident, but the company received more compliments about its handling than complaints.

QUEEN OF COQUITLAM—BURRARD DRYDOCK, OCTOBER 19, 1980

The most expensive accident—$3 million—occurred at Burrard Shipyards. The jumbo Queen of Coquitlam, *raised high in a floating drydock, crashed violently on her side when a support beam gave way. Both her engine room and the drydock were flooded. Leaning heavily against the dock wall, she threatened to roll over. Water caused an electrical short circuit and a small fire, but it was quickly brought under control. One crew member suffered a minor hand injury and the ship was saved. Another BC Ferry jumbo under construction was hastily towed out of the danger zone. Litigation over liability and damages was still continuing in 1985.*

Junior BC Ferries engineer, Bruno Schneider, was aboard at the time of the incident. It was early on a Sunday morning and the drydock was almost deserted. Schneider had the presence of mind to rush to the bridge. He shouted "Mayday, mayday" over a company marine radio band. The call was intercepted by Queen of Burnaby *out at sea. Relayed to Vancouver marine control, Kates tugboats were on the scene in minutes, tossing lines aboard to secure the ship.*

"This was a world first—a legitimate mayday call from a ship in drydock," said Jim Watson, BC Ferries engineering and construction chief.

After her sister's Gunboat Passage grounding, Queen of the North *was mobbed when she reached Port Hardy, carrying the rescued passengers.*

HER MAJESTY'S CORPORATION
CHAPTER EIGHT

"It's always more fun to be Caesar than to be God."—Stuart M. Hodgson, Chairman of the Board, BC Ferry Corporation (1981 -present)

The fare from Vancouver to Nanaimo aboard The Union Company's *S.S. Cutch* in 1890 was $2, a princely sum. Decades later, people were still paying $3.50 for round trips to the Sunshine Coast and other destinations aboard Union Steamships and the Canadian Pacific vessels. In 1976 on BC Ferries, the passenger fare to Nanaimo was still $2, and $1 on weekdays.

W.A.C. Bennett ran the provincial finances like a family's household budget. All that mattered to him, from a reporting point of view, was that the net worth was in good shape. If the mortgage was paid up, the future looked after with savings, and the basics attended to, then one could splurge on a holiday.

Similarly, in government, he boasted of being debt free, building a AAA credit rating and he told the public the numbers. It was not to him that one ledger item, in this case BC Ferries, may or may not be showing profit. He asked for and received sound economic management, but BC Ferries financial statements from the period are virtually meaningless. Substantial portions of company overhead were carried by other government departments. General manager Monty Aldous said the exhilarating growth made the first few years profitable, but non-stop spending on new ships and services through the 1960s changed the picture.

In 1960, Aldous set the base fares on the 24-mile Swartz Bay to Tsawwassen run at $2 for passengers and $5 for a car—cheap enough to attract business but low in comparison to similar-length ferry routes in Canada and abroad. When Black Ball was absorbed in 1961, the same fare was applied to the 31-mile journey in the north. As the decade progressed, comparative fares with Washington State, the new service in Alaska, CN Ferries in the Maritimes, and the hefty $30 and $40 price tags for shorter routes in Europe, justified a change. Aldous gathered his statistics together and went to see Premier Bennett. He argued for a fare increase from $2 to $3 on weekends, where backlogs were so routine people would pay anything, and the premier took it under advisement.

Days later, Aldous was figuratively knocked out of his office chair when word reached him that Premier Bennett had just announced to the legislature that weekday fares on the BC Ferries would be reduced from $2 to $1. "It was nothing more than a whim," Aldous said. But the price was to stick until 1976.

When the New Democratic Party came to power in 1972, their management approach to the ferries resembled the admiration of a beautiful flower that could prove poisonous to the touch. The province loved the ferries, small though the company was in comparison to hydro and social programs. There was no way on God's earth that fares would increase.

But former premier, Dave Barrett, remembers the serious lack of capacity in the system. "The traffic patterns were overwhelming." The principal ships were all stretched during the final years of W.A.C. Bennett's government, but it wasn't enough. "During his last years in power, W.A.C. refused to spend money on anything. We were running around the parliament buildings with pails to catch the dripping rain water," Barrett said.

The N.D.P. premier feared his government would be blamed for the interminable high season delays of up to seven hours. New ships were ordered.

Barrett recalls the ordering of three C-class super ferries was the only time in a 25-year political career that he was ever exposed to bribery. Highways Minister Bob Strachan brought an engine salesman to the premier's office. Choice of the mechanical plant would be a multi-million dollar decision. Barrett says that in the course of the conversation there was no doubt but that the salesman offered a heavy bribe to get the contract. "There wasn't enough evidence to call the cops, but there was enough for me to end the meeting right there," Barrett said.

A NEW ERA

When the government of W.A.C. Bennett fell in 1972, it was apparent to most observers that Monty Aldous' days were numbered. Although he had never been part of the Social Credit partisan politics, few people had been as close to W.A.C. Bennett. Charles Gallagher, who was hired to succeed Aldous, said that he, at one point, stressed to the N.D.P. government that Aldous was a public servant, not a politician, and would have to be retired with all the pension dignity implied by the definition. Aldous retired from the company he built in 1974. He would not be back in any capacity until 1981, when he would return in the statesman-like role of consultant.

Charles Gallagher brought BC Ferries international shipping experience. A business refugee from Nigeria's Biafran civil war, he moved his family to the tranquility of British Columbia, before scouting any job prospects. He was told repeatedly that he was over-qualified for whatever openings existed. But Gallagher was determined to stay and Gulf of Georgia Towing invented the position of "assistant to the president," at a salary of $500 a month. As the years passed, he became general manager of the tug and barge giant, Seaspan.

Meanwhile, the New Democratic Party government of British Columbia advertised for the position of BC Ferries General Manager. Forgetting his vow of many years past in Liverpool, Gallagher applied to the Public Services Commission and won the position. His Biafran experience would soon serve him well.

Charlie Gallagher walked into the middle of what 30-year coastal ferry veterans still regard as the worst year in their history—1974. It was apparent Monty Aldous was on the way out, but no one had told him. Bitterness still remained from the 1973 strike and the first collective agreement was in the process of negotiation, with the union firmly in the driver's seat. Traffic projections for the upcoming summer vastly exceeded the system's capacity. A cruise ship, *Stena Danica,* had arrived from Scandinavia to be converted for ferry use and the government was determined to "humanize" the summer service by hiring hundreds of college students to cheer up the terminals, carpenters to build planters and musicians to entertain. The summer was total chaos.

"When I arrived there was no handover of management....I just showed up. I went to see Monty myself. And I had to convince senior staff that I was not a hatchet man," Gallagher recalls. "I knew nothing about politics and very little about ferries."

The New Democratic Party can claim credit for expediting the Cowichan-class jumbo ferry construction and the first three ships were well under development by 1975. Charles Gallagher was, by then, firmly in charge. But the labor contract was starting to cause grief. Gallagher said that the pay raises, including perks, benefits and particularly the overtime provisions, combined to inflate the payroll by 50 percent overnight.

SOCIAL CREDIT RETURNS

When Bill Bennett, dubbed by the press as "Bennett The Younger," led Social Credit back to power at the end of 1975, the inadequate fare structure was finally addressed. If the price was ridiculous in the Aldous era, it reached the point of clear insanity by 1976. The hikes hit like a thunderclap, but the more important moves came in management structure. The $100 million operation could no longer be run family style.

Gallagher, improperly viewed by some members of the new government as an N.D.P. political appointment, was unable to endear himself to his new masters with cheerful news. He told his minister, Jack Davis, that 1976 could produce a deficit as high as $67 million if dramatic action was not soon taken. The government acted with a vengeance—fares were doubled, routes were cut back, dining rooms were eliminated. Through it all, Charles Gallagher took much of the heat. Although traffic volume fell substantially, the deficit was reduced to $15 million.

Most Social Credit strategists, using hindsight, now say they should have made the changes more gently, but in fact almost ten years earlier, Monty Aldous had failed in attempts to convince W.A.C. Bennett to raise fares. And Aldous says to this day that the table service dining rooms were crucial in the beginning for "image" purposes, but didn't belong in an efficient ferry system.

Although the fare and service changes were most visible to the public and therefore most controversial, the hallmark of the Bill Bennett-style of government was to have a more profound impact on the fleet—autonomous management through an independent Crown

One of the more innovative decisions during the New Democratic Party's period in power (1972-1975) was the arrival from Europe of a cruise ship styled ferry, Stena Danica *(top right)*.

The NDP's Minister of Transportation and Communications, Robert Strachan (top left) is shown at the rechristening of the ship as Queen of Surrey.

Renamed Queen of the North, *she was designated "flagship" of the fleet in 1985.*

Corporation. It had been discussed for years and, finally, its day had come. BC Ferries would stand alone.

The most urgent need was for a money man and he was dicovered in Edmonton. Joe Estock, a veteran of the Yukon and White Pass Railway, had been with Max Ward since 1964, as Wardair's vice-president of finance. By 1976, Estock's wife, a Victoria native, was anxious to come home. Joe Estock became the BC Ferries chief financial officer and, subsequently, assistant general manager of finance.

The British Columbia Ferry Corporation went into business on January 1, 1977.

AUTONOMY

During his years running the company, Charles Gallagher supervised a capital expansion program, both ships and terminals, totalling almost $200 million. He managed the advent of the Crown Corporation, requiring substantial growth of head office with expertise in finance, personnel, planning, law and associated fields. Much had been previously done by other government departments.

One of his most inspired management moves is still widely misunderstood by both the public and the Opposition in the Legislature. As the Crown Corporation took shape, financing the three Cowichan-class vessels, *Queen of Cowichan, Queen of Coquitlam* and *Queen of Alberni,* was a major concern.

The investment firm of McLeod, Young and Weir came to Gallagher with a proposal widely used in aviation and shipping circles. Get "angels" to own the ships—unknown investors. As a non-profit Crown Corporation, BC Ferries could not depreciate the expensive ships against income tax, but if others, through a giant trust company, owned the vessels, they could write it all off from other income over three years. Several major trust houses became the owners of record and the Crown Corporation leased the ships back for seventeen years at a rental of 7.4 percent—a full two percentage points under the market value.

The investors accepted less interest on their money, but they enjoyed the huge tax write-off. The transaction was approximately $50 million. With the payment of 15 percent of mortgage value during the mid-1990s, the ships will revert to unqualified provincial ownership. The direct cash saving to British Columbia will be as much as $20 million—essentially one free ship. Today, each of the three ships would cost over $40 million to build.

The deal was so startlingly successful that the federal government changed the tax laws so that future "angels" could only deduct such investments from income gained from the industry in question—in this case, shipping. BC Ferries has since not been able to use the device.

NEW DIRECTIONS

Gallagher ran BC Ferries as if it was a private business. He would accept no other mandate. He sometimes didn't appear to understand why it was a government entity. As much as observers give him credit for considerable achievements in construction, finance and building the corporation, they also talk of his failure in both staff and public relations. Many captains complained that they never once saw him on their bridge in the entire seven-year era.

By 1981, morale within the fleet was at an all-time low and Gallagher was fighting with several members of his board of directors. He was opposed to the government's emerging policy of giving the board a geographic complexion: people to represent different regions of the province. He believed the board should consist only of the best shipping and transport finance specialists available.

Both Alex Fraser—Minister of Transportation and Highways, and Chairman of the Board of BC Ferries—and Gallagher as chief executive officer looked forwad to the day when the company, like other Crown Corporations, would have a chairman independent of the cabinet. When it was announced that Stuart M. Hodgson was to become chairman of the board, Gallagher was, initially, pleased. He had long argued that the board of directors should be arms-length

THE MOUSE THAT ROARED

In 1974, Britain's mighty Peninsular and Oriental Steam Navigation Company purchased Princess Cruises of Seattle, and its renowned cruise ship Island Princess, *the original "Love Boat" of T.V. fame. (The T.V. show features the structurally identical* Pacific Princess, *but insiders have always known her sister to be superior.) When P&O attempted to transfer* Island Princess' *registry from Norwegian to British, government officials in London advised that it could not be done. BC Ferries had a ship of that name. The doughty-little catamaran-hulled, 49-car* Island Princess, *bobbing her way around the north tip of Vancouver Island at the time, had never known such attention.*

The vessel had originally been built for Sparky New's Coast Ferries, but she came into the BC Ferries fleet in 1969, soon after to become yet another subject for engineering creativity. Island Princess *was sliced in half both vertically and horizontally. Her widened deck was stretched over a new catamaran hull configuration. The horizontal slice was welded back together after the insertion of a new deck of passenger accommodations. The vessel then went into service connecting the forest industry town of Port Hardy at the north tip of Vancouver Island with the northern extremity of the Island Highway. When a new highway forged through to Port Hardy in the late 1970s, the ferry service was no longer necessary and Port Hardy became the southern gateway of BC Ferries' northern service.*

But little Island Princess *was still in her heyday when the great P&O Line went to see Charles Gallagher in Victoria and, with much levity, suggested this impasse could surely be settled in a gentlemanly way. It could not. The offer of money was then discussed. This was unacceptable. After keeping his guests in suspense, Gallagher finally advised them that P&O had been sailing to British Columbia for decades, and yet there was not one single momento in Victoria's Maritime Museum. The result was a beautiful model of the historic ship* Arcadia *and an assortment of P&O memorabilia for the museum. Instantly, BC Ferries had a new vessel:* North Island Princess.

YEARS OF TRANSITION

"There is no one I respect more than Charlie Gallagher."—Norm Thornber, BC Ferries union executive and subsequently Manager, Labor Relations.

Stuart Hodgson, who was to succeed Charles Gallagher as Chief Executive Officer of BC Ferries, describes his predecessor's era (1974-1981) with empathy, "These were years of transition—very diffiuclt years."

Gallagher had been in shipping since he was sixteen, starting as a clerk in a customs brokerage in his native Liverpool. After a 15-month tour with the Royal Air Force, including the Suez crisis, he returned home to work for the Mersey Docks and Harbors Board. In an executive capacity with the board, he became totally frustrated by political meddling. "I swore then that I'd never work for a government corporation again."

Returning to the private sector, he was posted by the Guinea Gulf Lines to become assistant cargo superintendent in Ghana and, subsequently, Lagos, Nigeria, just in time for the Biafran civil war. As rumbles from the interior told of fierce fighting, Gallagher scrambled to keep the cargo and vessels under his control out of the hands of rebels. He was appointed "area warden" for a section of geography near his port town.

"It was an area about twice the size of the Lower Mainland," he said. An evacuation plan was devised for the foreign community. "Then we saw these guys walking in with sub-machine guns, ragged trousers and bare feet." Gallagher remembers thinking how grateful he was that a son's illness in England had forced him to leave the family behind.

As he was on the phone to his company headquarters in Britain one day, a group of drum-beating natives, faces painted with whitewash, stormed into his office. "I thought I was a goner," he remembers. But the incident passed and he soon stole away in the dead of night aboard a tramp steamer, determined that his would be an end to his days of adventure. It was August, 1967.

Gallagher enjoyed some time with his family in Liverpool before deciding to explore opportunities in Canada. He traveled from Montreal west, finally arriving on the shores of English Bay. "I walked out of the Sylvia Hotel and said, 'That's it folks—this where I want my family to be.'"

from government.

It was only after Hodgson arrived that it was made clear that the new chairman was also to be chief executive officer. Fraser, as minister responsible, would sit as a board member and report on behalf of the corporation to government. Gallagher was offered the opportunity to continue as general manager, but he saw it as a definite demotion. "Gentlemen, what you have given me is an instructed dismissal," he says he advised the board. The formal words to the directors were precisely, "You have conceptually terminated my position." A parting settlement was soon negotiated.

His era ended as it began. Now back as an executive with Seaspan, Gallagher harbors no bitterness. "I am damn proud of what we did at BC Ferries." The man who was to succeed him couldn't possibly have been more different in style and background.

Charles Gallagher, at the opening of Bear Cove Terminal, Port Hardy, in 1979.

THE SHIP CUTTERS' RETURN

Ships must view the engineering department of BC Ferries with the same degree of affection that a frog has for a biology lab. The cutters were at it again in 1984, and this time Queen of Alberni was under the knife. The $9 million expansion was a pet project of the Hodgson era. The ship was sliced in half horizontally, and an entire new car deck was inserted, increasing automobile capacity from 145 to 300.

A unique member of the jumbo family, Alberni's design was to service tractor trailers and overheight vehicles. Her hull and engineering plant were the same as her C-Class sisters, but the car deck remained a vast open cavern, and the passenger accommodation space was substantially less. But she lacked versatility. Thus, a plan unfolded to retain all her overheight capability, but to add a car deck. The design was an in-house job under engineering boss Jim Watson, naval architect Tom Blyth and construction superintendant Peter Mehta. Burrard Yarrows did the work.

It had been hoped that the renovated Queen of Alberni would serve the Sunshine Coast, but local residents protested her restricted passenger space. Also, midway through 1985, a renewed economy brought unpredicted demand for additional tractor-trailer capacity between Nanaimo and the mainland, reducing the need for her extra car deck.

"CALL ME 'STU' "

Stuart Hodgson

Stuart Hodgson was born in Vancouver April 1, 1924. After graduating from John Oliver High School, he went to work loading trucks at a lumber mill. "They believed in a great strong back and a weak head. I had both," he told an interviewer in 1985. When the war broke out, he marked time until he was old enough to join the navy. Finally, he served on corvettes in Atlantic and Murmansk convoy duty for three years, rising to the rank of Acting Petty Officer by 1945.

Returning home to a job at Vancouver Plywood, Hodgson soon became involved in a monumental battle to oust communists from executive positions within the International Woodworkers of America. Subsequent successful efforts guided the union into an era of both sophistication and public respect. His career as a labor leader took him to the highest offices provincially, nationally and, upon occasion, internationally.

"In those days (circa 1950), unions weren't very popular, and I know my family and my relatives thought that I'd gone bad. It was second only to going to jail," Hodgson said.

He first went north in 1964, asked by the federal government to be a consultant in labor relations. Shortly after his arrival, the deputy commissioner of The Territories was felled by a heart attack while preparing the annual budget. Hodgson was asked to pinch-hit and he put the budget together in three days. Impressed, the commissioner offered him the position of full-time deputy. Hodgson, his wife Pearl, son and daughter moved to Yellowknife and, in 1967, he was called into the office of Prime Minister Lester B. Pearson who advised him that he was to be appointed commissioner. "I told him I didn't know anything about government and he said that was why he wanted me to do it," Hodgson said.

In his twelve years as commissioner, Hodgson made bold strides, advancing levels of democratic input and organization, from a colonial-style management conducted largely by the RCMP, to a streamlined network throughout the north's diversity of people and geography. He became a friend of Prime Minister Pierre Elliot Trudeau, always proud to mention his association even when, in later years at home in British Columbia, it was certain to produce an argument.

In 1979, Hodgson says he and Pearl "were beginning to feel the cold." When Prime Minister Trudeau proposed that they move to Ottawa to assist in sorting out a variety of problems in Canada-U.S. relations, he jumped at the chance, but the parting from Yellowknife was tearful and, to this day, the mere mention of the north brings a twinkle to his eye.

As a permanent member of the International Joint Commission, Hodgson was to spend two years traveling between Ottawa and Washington, D.C. from the offices of the Prime Minister and Governor-General, to that of the U.S. Secretary of State. He enjoyed full ambassadorial status. During the course of his long federal service, Hodgson was awarded the highest civilian honor in the country: Officer of the Order of Canada.

By 1981, the treaties he was working on with the Americans were largely completed. Some of the I.J.C. work had brought him back to his native British Columbia. Each trip increased his desire to stay. When a representative of the provincial government proposed that he return to run the ferry system, he soon made a courtesy call on Prime Minister Trudeau, advising him that he would like to accept. Trudeau wished him well and, after almost two decades, Stu Hodgson came home.

THE HOMECOMING

It has been described by more than one political observer as the most inspired appointment in the ten years of Premier Bill Bennett's government. On the first day at work, Hodgson bounded around the ferry corporation office announcing, "My name's Hodgson, call me 'Stu'—I don't know anything about ferries."

Journalist Bob Hunter, in a 1985 *Equity* magazine article, described him as "a mountain of friendly man." Burly, amiable and gravel-voiced, Stuart M. Hodgson has a natural gift for negotiation and public relations, but he also demands solid homework and precision. Shortly after his arrival on the BC Ferries scene, a colleague asked a Hodgson friend, "Is he for real or full of baloney?" The friend chuckled, "You might describe it that way, but Stu has turned it into an art form—the highest level of diplomacy, the stuff of great ambassadorial talents. . . .In his hands, humility becomes a lethal weapon."

All of those skills and more would be needed at BC Ferries.

Premier Bennett remembers that the morale at the time was devastated. Serious disagreements prevailed between the board of directors and the company management. The first sensations of a painful recession were being felt in failing traffic and revenues. But costs were spiralling upward and the union contract, largely unchanged since 1974, continued to make the system almost unmanageable. Two of the largest ships were tied up with cracks in the engine plating.

Hodgson replaced Highways Minister Alex Fraser as chairman of the board and Charles Gallagher as chief executive officer. Engineering superintendent George Baldwin was promoted to general manager, and the structure of management was redesigned with four assistant general managers—operations, finance, engineering and human resources. All but two of the key positions were promotions from within the company. Hodgson brought in a former colleague from Yellowknife days, Rod Morrison, to head human resources, responsible for personnel, labor relations and, particu-

larly, seminars and counselling aimed at improving morale; and, a French-Canadian lady, Carmen Laurin, an associate from I.J.C. activities, to set up sophisticated systems of reporting and research.

Upon his return to British Columbia, Hodgson says he was amazed at how big the ferry system had become, but he was appalled at the lack of accountability throughout the company. "You must have faith in people—a guy has got to be allowed to make mistakes. We designed a system based on responsibility, authority and accountability. Each guy has a little to contribute, some more than others," he said.

At first he traveled on the ships talking to people. Several captains informed him that they found it embarrassing in the cafeterias if they had to supply cash for food when they entertained visitors. Hodgson was flabbergasted and at the next management meeting, the policy was changed. There was a fear that captains might abuse the privilege if the food was free. "I said that this was unbelievable. We would trust a man with a $30 million ship but we couldn't trust him with a hamburger! . . .The policy changed on the spot," Hodgson said.

Travels throughout the province convinced him that the public had little understanding about the personnel of the ferry system, or the complexities of the many positions from top to bottom. As a by-product of managerial insensitivity and internal union discord, too many staff members had developed a low image of themselves and a jaded perspective of the corporation. Therefore, he devised a plan in co-operation with Andy McKechnie and the BC Ferry and Marine Workers Union to launch a television, poster and other media campaign showing employees performing their diverse tasks. The theme of the media blitz was *Skill, Competence, Heart.*

GREAT WHITE FATHER

It was a blustery day in the spring of 1969 at the Resolute airstrip on Cornwallis Island, some 600 miles north of the Arctic Circle. A group of native leaders was huddled at the side of the runway watching a small aircraft taxi away from them. Asked by a fellow spectator who was aboard the plane, an Inuit replied, "Great White Father." Perplexed, the visitor repeated the question. The Eskimo elaborated, "The government!"

The aircraft was transporting Stuart Milton Hodgson, Commissioner of The Northwest Territories from 1967 to 1979. The N.W.T. has a full third of Canada's land mass and most of the country's awesome arctic icecap. The Inuit leader was not exaggerating. In the north, the federally-appointed commissioner embraces both the vice-regal duties of a provincial lieutenant-governor and the executive responsibilities of a premier.

In the vice-regal aspect of his role as Northwest Territories Commissioner, Stu Hodgson hosted the Royal Family on numerous occasions, developing friendships that have led to frequent social calls on Buckingham Palace. He says that the Queen, but particularly the Duke of Edinburgh and Prince Charles were quickly charmed by the romance and majesty of the north. The men were quick to avail themselves of opportunities to fish, study wildlife and enjoy other adventures.

One charming anecdote made the pages of Reader's Digest. Hodgson was hosting Queen Elizabeth and Prince Philip on a multi-stop air journey across the vast landscape. At each airstrip, Hodgson's role was to climb out the rear door of the plane and run to the foot of the front steps. Once there, with local dignitaries, the Royal Party would emerge and the commissioner would conduct the formal welcome. At one stop, as Hodgson dashed from the rear door, he slipped and fell in the mud. By the time he had recovered and had partially brushed off the dirt, the Queen and The Duke were awaiting his arrival. When Hodgson puffed up to them, Her Majesty smiled and said, "We beat you this time!"

On another occasion at the community of Fort Providence, the Royal Party was traveling by motorcade and Hodgson, also required to be the official greeter at each stop, would ease out the door of his vehicle at the rear of the procession and, at about an eighth of a mile from the destination, he'd jump from the slowly-moving car and run toward the receiving line. Prior to each stop, he'd carefully read, from a meticulous program, the names of the people he was to introduce.

At For Providence, there was to be one Catholic priest and a nun. As he started his run from the car, he gasped, and gagged on a mouthful of black flies when he saw the priest with three nuns. As the Queen and Prince Philip emerged from their limousine, Hodgson was still choking on the flies. He strained to blurt out the priest's name and asked him to introduce the nuns with him. "As the Royal Couple went past, the Queen looked at me very strangely—I was still choking on the flies." Finally, at the rear of the procession, Princess Anne came by, pausing to whisper in the Commissioner's ear. "How did they taste?"

H.R.H. Prince Charles, gets an inspection tour of the North, by the North-West Territories Commissioner Stuart Hodgson.

YEARS OF CONSOLIDATION

Hodgson describes the Monty Aldous era as "the formative years—the most exciting years." He says Charles Gallagher's period was the "years of transition" when the company grew up. His own period, he calls the "years of consolidation," when strong management systems and firm bottom-line fiscal responsiblity were imposed.

But the ravages of the recession and the need for restraint impaired efforts to improve morale. The two main routes across Georgia Strait have become profitable once again, but all the thirteen other routes lose money, a marine highway public service represented by an annual government subsidy. The government grant steadily climbed through the 1970s and early 1980s, peaking at $58.9 million in 1982. Determined efforts by the corporation at efficiency and restraint, have reduced the annual allotment to $40 million.

Hodgson's efforts have achieved harmony and effectiveness within the board of directors and the respect of his political superiors. The public image of both the corporation and its employees have been substantially improved. But, as the recession deepened, over 200 layoffs became necessary along with a cutback in frequency of service. The layoffs were tough in themselves, but the affected employees invoked seniority clauses in their contract and about 400 "bumps" took place. People were moving from job to job, causing enormous disruption.

Stu Hodgson is, however, grateful for the co-operation shown by the BC Ferry and Marine Workers' Union and hopeful that Expo 86 and a generally improved economy will get everyone back to work. This would touch off a new round of promotions and a new era of pride and enthusiasm within the company.

ON THE BUSES

At the height of an agonizing two-month bus strike in Vancouver and Victoria in 1984, it mystified observers that one of Canada's most renowned labor leaders, Joe Morris—most frequently asso-ciated through his career with the New Democratic Party—had accepted a Social Credit government invitation to mediate the dispute. It should have been obvious that the subtle hand of Stuart M. Hodgson was at work somewhere in the back rooms of transit policy making. Morris, a friend from the the old days of the International Woodworkers of America, had earlier accepted a position on the BC Ferries Board of Directors.

When the Legislature finally ordered the buses back to work, it was announced that Hodgson was to take over transit management, including the construction of a one-billion-dollar rapid transit system. He resigned as Chief Executive Officer of BC Ferries, but he remained as Chairman of the Board. "There is still a tremendous amount of work to be done," he said.

At dawn, the day after the announcement, Hodgson traveled to the Victoria transit headquarters, joining the early morning shift of bus drivers in their locker room. "Hi," he said, "My name's Hodgson—call me 'Stu'—and I don't know a darn thing about buses."

"Follow the Birds to Victoria"

THE SUMMER OF '74

The summer of 1974 proved to be disastrous. It was the second year of the New Democratic Party's management of the ferries. A year before, with an unfortunate strike coupled with a shortage of capacity and exploding traffic demands, concern became as much a matter of politics as transportation. The N.D.P. was determined to "humanize" the ferries.

Musicians descended upon the ships to entertain passengers. The government wanted to hire students from music schools but soon ran smack into its historic partnership with trade unions: the Musicians' Union got the jobs. Carpenters showed up at all the terminals to construct benches, cedar planters and hanging baskets. Veteran employees spent the summer treating basket-assault concussions.

But it was the instant employment of hundreds of students that created the greatest levels of chaos. The youngsters provided tourists with helpful hints, pitched in wherever they could, and chauffeured a new fleet of hastily rented golf carts and mini-vans. These transported elderly and handicapped people to ferry elevators before other traffic could begin loading. As cars in the terminal waiting lines stretched into the horizon and beyond, and captains paced the ships' bridges, the youngsters had a field day whizzing around the car decks.

Horseshoe Bay terminal agent Ken Johnson, a Black Ball veteran, said it was the worst summer of his life. His normal staff of 65 people had doubled overnight. He had to monitor and find work for 60 young people. One day he remembers calling down to his yard foreman enquiring whether all the students had shown up for work. "Hell, I don't know," the beleagured foreman replied. "There's a few of them up on the cliff smoking pot. I see a couple necking under a tree on the beach ....hell, they are all over the place." Toward the end of the summer, Johnson handed in a letter of resignation. His boss, Frank Ramsay, ordered him to take a two-week vacation. By September, everything returned to normal and the resignation was forgotten.

At one point, head office started getting complaints about a well-endowed young girl at Swartz Bay Terminal who became a bra-less distraction. Agent Denny Keen was ordered to tell her to wear a bra. A gentleman of the old school, Keen protested that he couldn't discuss such things with a young lady. But orders were orders and he called her into the office. He told her to come to work the next day, "with your uppers on." The girl apparently got the message. Keen reported, "She is now wearing the correct things."

THE BUM RAP

While the N.D.P. was in power, W.A.C. Bennett received a rude notice advising him that his lifetime pass on the BC Ferries had been revoked. The blame, naturally, focused immediately on the scallywags who had dared defeat him at the polls. His son, Premier Bill Bennett, remembers that his father took no notice of the revocation. "He'd roll up to the terminal booth, hold out his canceled pass, and advise the attendant, 'Here's my pass. . . . Number One!' No one had the heart to deny him."

Unknown to either of the Bennetts was the obsession BC Ferries General Manager Charles Gallagher had about not granting passes. To this day, when you talk to his close associates about his era at the company, it doesn't take long before the subject of passes comes up. It is doubtful he ever intended to cut off W.A.C. Bennett, but several times he issued edicts that every pass be canceled—MLAs, executives, pensioners, old friends—a broad brush.

"Equality for all, privilege for none," Gallagher said in a 1985 interview. In fact, he used W.A.C. Bennett to justify his move. The fomer premier would pull rank only in the case of official business. Salt Spring Islanders fondly remember Mrs. Bennett brewing tea and handing out sandwiches from a picnic hamper, as she and her husband patiently waited in line for a ferry.

The standard prerequisite within every passenger transportation organization in the world is an anathema to Charles Gallagher. He says his British father was retired from the railway after a life of service with a starvation pension. But management arrogantly gave him a lifetime travel pass as if it was a crown jewel. "Our people enjoy top level pensions," Gallagher says. "They can afford to pay for their own travel. And if we are to operate like a private business, why should the politicians and their cronies get free passage?"

Before Gallagher's departure, the board of directors had managed to reinstate most pass privileges, and after the change of management, the job was completed.

One of Bill Bennett's first acts after becoming premier was to present his predecessor, Dave Barrett, with a lifetime pass on the ferries. Although he still thinks Bennett was "rubbing it in," Barrett says the pass is one of the most prized mementos of his political career.

SHIP PEOPLE
CHAPTER NINE

"In the cruise ship world, the greatest ocean the crews ever cross is the gulf between the ships and head office."—The author, at a 1984 BC Ferries seminar.

The late Captain Paddy "Hard Over" Hannigan, one of the great characters in ferry annals, was touring the bridge of a new ship one day with a company executive. He looked at the bridge controls and remarked, "The handles are too short." The boss was mystified until Hannigan grinned, "Because you won't be able to reach them from head office."

Hannigan earned his nickname because of the enthusiasm with which he'd boom his commands, "Hard a' port" or "Hard a' starboard," startling a good many helmsman in his day. He was also noted for never physically touching the perpetual cigarette dangling from his mouth. Ashes would fall leisurely on his double-breasted uniform, soon to be smudged into an unsightly mess. About halfway through each shift, Hannigan would reverse the buttons on his jacket, burying the stains inside.

Press files on a shipping company distort reality through a preponderance of accident stories. Similarly, the media picture of BC Ferries as a troubled labor environment is one of the great myths of British Columbia life. However, it is not surprising in a company born out of a labor crisis, and with the almost neurotic insecurity on the islands about transportation links. The prevailing attitude, though, is an insult both to the union and management.

Over its 25-year life, BC Ferries has been on strike for twenty-two days. There have been several minor skirmishes when other people's picket lines had to be respected. In a 1985 interview, Premier Bill Bennett said, "Our ferry workers have not been the ones who have caused us problems."

The salaries in the fleet are good. There are no full-time employees earning less than $20,000 a year, and the scale rises to chief engineers and masters in the $50,000 range. Only the very top executives of the corporation exceed that figure, and they don't enjoy the added remuneration from overtime. The fringe benefits are as good or better than those enjoyed by any organized work force.

From the deck and engine officers through the ranks of seamen and catering staff, there is not a so-called "unskilled" permanent position aboard BC Ferry ships. All crew require specialized lifeboat and fire safety tickets in addition to their specific job abilities. The photos show bridge officers at work, and a routine lifeboat drill.

Captain Al Bahry (below) outlines procedures to Alex Fraser, the Minister of Transportation and Highways.

The major staffing problem that has frustrated sound economic management has not been wages but working conditions. Items such as obligatory stand-by days with whole crews doing very little during a shift, or the 7.5-hour day at sea guaranteeing a half hour of double time for all crew every day. These have been slowly whittled down by management in more recent negotiations.

The excesses of the 1974 contract put added money in everyone's pocket, but it also forced an earthquake of corporate decisions that have made hundreds of positions redundant—much larger ships increasing capacity far more than staff, elimination of dining rooms, cutbacks in service and recession-era layoffs. From an employment peak of over 3,000 employees, the company now operates effectively with between 2,000 and 2,500, depending on the season.

BC FERRY & MARINE WORKERS' UNION

Building a union out of the debris of the 1958 calamity that forced government's direct intervention in the ferry business, was almost an impossible assignment. The government enjoyed all the anti-union public support it needed to start a ferry system. BC Ferries original officers remained members of the Canadian Merchant Service Guild, without official bargaining status, but all other employees understood that they were without representation when they signed aboard. When the government advertised for employees in 1960, there were 2,000 applications for fewer than 190 positions.

When the Black Ball Line was taken over, the government inherited trade union agreements, but it was made clear to labor that strikes would not be tolerated. Since BC Ferries salaries were largely in concert with Black Ball at the beginning, it was a non-issue. But soon, the Black Ball people fell under precisely the same rules as everyone else in the fleet. Their unions became part of history.

But there were grievances in the early years that caused the first signs of organized resistance. The leaders were the late George Hornett in Victoria and in Nanaimo, a pugnacious native of

Hamilton, Ontario, Norm Thornber, who had served overseas with the navy four years during the war, migrating west shortly thereafter. He worked in a series of jobs—bartender, advertising and real estate sales—until being hired by BC Ferries in 1963 as a dining room steward based in Nanaimo. He wasn't on the job for long, listening to the grievances of fellow employees, before he started advocating the formation of a union.

Many of his colleagues, wearing scars from labor scraps of the late 1950s and fearing W.A.C. Bennett's ferocious determination never again to let a union threaten the security of transportation to Vancouver Island, were less than enthusiastic. However, he found a soul-mate in George Hornett and organizational efforts continued on both major routes of the system.

Thornber said working conditions and wages were appalling. No grievance procedure, people were dismissed without appeal, no pensions and "crazy hours of work"—sixteen days on and three days off, and frequently fifteen and sixteen hours' work a day. The company often insisted that vacations take place only when an employee's ship went in for annual refit, and sometimes the work schedule might entail a sixty-day period (less days off) on mornings and sixty days on evenings. Overtime was paid 1.2 times the usual hourly wage, but only after an employee had accumulated 2,008 hours worked in a given calendar year, regardless of how long he worked on any one day.

Immigration from the British Isles was free and easy in those years and usually even the most meagre Canadian salaries looked attractive to them, Thornber remembers. "The company was predominantly British with reason—an almost inexhaustible supply of cheap labor."

Thornber, Hornett and the fledgling union they formed struggled without success to win recognition from the government. Instead, they signed up 600 members into the British Columbia Government Employees' Association, but soon had a fight with them and withdrew for the entire year 1964. In 1965 the ferry workers were back in the B.C.G.E.A. fold. Thornber recalls, "We paid a per capita for them to keep their noses out of our affairs, but they had the recognition."

Meanwhile, partly because of efforts to unify employees from the diverse components of the merged ferry services and especially because of the first threat of union organization, the government struck a plan to make all ferry employees civil servants. Top executives traveled through the terminals, offices and ships, carrying Bibles, getting everyone to swear allegiance to the Crown. The employees were sold on the basis of civil service security and benefits, at the time thought to be a sinecure for life. But, as history unveiled, it became apparent that it was merely an anti-union tactic: civil servants were not permitted to strike.

In these early years, the BC Ferry & Marine Workers' Union consisted of what became known as "unlicensed" personnel. The "licensed" people were the officers, who were mostly members of The Guild. Without automatic dues check off by the employer, it was difficult to keep the union afloat. There were no salaries for the union executive and, in fact, shop stewards had to collect the dues on the spot, going from member to member. But the union persisted in pressing its point and, despite the government's determined efforts to prevent the ferry unionization, Thornber said the government never made any strike-breaking attempts—neither threats, firings nor impossible transfers.

"They were so sure of themselves," he said.

THE STRIKE OF 1968

The ferry workers shocked the government and indeed the province by showing solidarity in a two-week 1968 strike. The government cried that it was "illegal," which, technically, it was, since there was no recognized union.

It was a true donnybrook. As the strike was threatened, Phil Gaglardi convinced W.A.C. Bennett to let him take charge. Gaglardi said the ferry employees had violated their oath and once it was made clear to them that dismissal could be immediate, they would dutifully file back to work.

When it was determined by the government that a strike was imminent, the British Columbia Ferry Authority was formally dissolved. Everything and everybody was transferred to the Department of Highways. In a legal sense, the ferries would remain a branch of the highways ministry until 1977, but, in practice, the autonomous operation never changed at all. It was a labor relations ploy.

At the start of the 1968 ferry shutdown, the highways minister called a meeting in the Hotel Vancouver with the ferry workers. "Gaglardi stressed the civil service oath and told us that if employees were not back to work the next day, they would all be fired," Thornber recalls. "Our group met until 5 a.m., had a sing song, and finally we said, 'to hell with them' and we all went home."

As the ships remained idle, every employee received a telegram conveying an ultimatum: Go to work or be fired. This produced reactions ranging from concern to confusion and finally, to outright hilarity. But the strike held and W.A.C. Bennett is reported to have called in Highways Minister Gaglardi to ask, "Do you have any more great ideas Phil?"

When the strike ended after two weeks, the union had made great strides in money, working conditions and, perhaps most importantly, recognition. The government fell a long way short of approving collective bargaining, but it agreed to collect dues from the payroll and allow the union to circulate its bulletins with the pay cheques. An employees association was recognized for the purpose of discussing working conditions.

Thornber remembers that the union had exactly $12.37 in the bank at the end of the strike. The first membership cards for the BC Ferry and Marine Workers' Union were run off on a church Gestetner machine. "When everything was agreed with Les Peterson (Labor Minister), we tossed in one item at the end—we asked for ferry passes for our union business agents. He thought it was nothing and instantly said yes. For us, absolutely broke, it was a godsend. . . . We never looked back after that."

THE STRIKE OF 1973

In 1972 the New Democratic Party came to power and everyone in the public service, including the ferry workers, was looking forward to promised full collective bargaining. But the events of Norm Thornber's first meeting with N.D.P. minister Bob Strachan in 1973 came as a complete shock. The minister opened the meeting by announcing that a deal had been struck with John Fryer of the British Columbia Government Employees Union which would be binding on all public servants: a $75-a-month pay raise across the board, which would have the effect of giving the people at the bottom a higher percentage increase.

The ferry workers, whose relations with the B.C.G.E.U. and the B.C.G.E.A. before it were strained at the best of times, were outraged and insulted because they weren't consulted. Stressing the independence of his small union, business agent Thornber said he told Strachan, "We will settle for $70, or we will settle for $80, but we will not settle for anything Fryer negotiates." Strachan said it was firm government policy. Thornber stormed from the meeting with the warning, *"This is going to cost you!"*

The BC Ferry and Marine Workers' Union went on strike at the height of the tourist season of 1973 with a list of demands which Thornber described as endless. "We threw everything in we could think of." Less than a week later, the government caved in, agreeing to do just about everything.

"I had a gun to my head," Strachan later told broadcaster Jack Webster, a phrase that will not be forgotten in the history of BC Ferries. By the time collective bargaining had become law and the first master agreement of the ferry workers came into place in 1974, one British Columbia Federation of Labor official described it as, "A labor leader's heaven." There was nothing—no conceivable benefit—left out of the contract. It became a fiscal nightmare for management, particularly a clause guaranteeing a 7.5-hour day with a full double time for overtime. One minute over a scheduled shift paid a full half hour of overtime. As the ferry watches worked four two-hour sailings a day (and frequently up to 10-hour shifts on the Nanaimo run), overtime became unavoidable for every ship employee, every day.

The concensus among all those involved at the time—Monty Aldous and Charles Gallagher for management, Thornber for the union, and one top-level N.D.P. cabinet member who chose not to be identified out of respect for the memory of the late Bob Strachan—was simply that Strachan "panicked."

"He could have settled that thing and saved money," Thornber said. "It was embarrassing to us because most of our people were members of the party."

Aldous said he told the government that a strike was not necessary. But when Strachan dug in his heels, the general manager said he advised the government, "If there is going to be a strike, I want your assurance that you are not going to give in." Strachan gave in and it was worse when the contract was formalized in 1974. "That was the frightening thing—they just gave away everything," said Aldous. Charles Gallagher recalls, "They gave the barn away."

At the height of his glory, his members basking in comforts they couldn't have imagined five years earlier, Thornber entered his toughest days. Relations with the BC Government Employees Union and John Fryer couldn't have been worse. The new government of Bill Bennett forged extensive cutbacks in service, personnel requirements and style of management, all creating turbulence within the union. In 1978, militant union members deposed the executive and the newly elected officers fired business agent Norm Thornber. Partially in revenge, he ended his ferry days as the BC Ferries Manager of Labor Relations, going head to head against the union members who had disenfranchised him.

THE FERRY FAMILY

At the height of a ferry shutdown and in its aftermath, an inconvenienced public knows no bounds of decency in personal slurs cast at employees. Officers are called "bus drivers," catering people are known as "pie-slicers" and others take great pains in advising that terminal staff do little all day but lean against the poles. Salaries, already good by any shipping comparison, get inflated in the public mind to such esoteric heights that employees' family members suspect that all the wages don't come home.

What the public frequently misunderstands is that much more is expected from ferry employees than their visible functions. A

The bridge of Queen of Victoria *(top left), with Chief Officer Bill Plant and Captain Ray Calberg at the controls.*

BC Ferries personnel at the historic peak went over the 3,000 mark, but larger ships and cost efficiencies have reduced the high season total to about 2,500. The jobs are as diverse as in any complicated industrial concern.

cleaner, cashier, or steward, also has formal certification as a seaman, fully trained in all emergency procedures. When periodically it has been suggested that BC Ferries contract out food services, it is not understood that this likely wouldn't save a penny. Transport Canada safety standards dictate the minimum crew required for safety reasons and they must be certified. A concessionaire would either bring aboard surplus staff, increasing costs, or would have to qualify everyone as a seaman. Wages would soon reflect the effort.

Canadian Coast Guard regulations require that 75 percent of BC Ferries crews, on any given sailing, have lifeboat and fire safety certificates. Because of the nature of the route system, with ships frequently in open waters, lifeboats or liferafts are required for all passengers and crew. The crew must be trained to handle them. Washington State Ferries, by comparison, are considered to be in constantly sheltered waters and relatively close to a shoreline. U.S. authorities allow the company to satisfy safety needs with a preponderance of life jackets. This demands a trained crew that can be less than half BC Ferries' requirement. It leaves Washington State with the luxury of contracting out food services to the best bidder.

It is an amazing sight to watch BC Ferries crews go through their firefighting and boat drill routines. Tiny middle-aged ladies toss around the life jackets and heavy equipment with the ease of old tars. A Chinese cleaner or cook wields a fire hose like a pro, incongruously dressed in the space-like safety gear.

Some days are more impressive than others. One day an officer took a crew out in a lifeboat equipped with a "Flemming Gear," a large stick between the legs of each crew member. The boat is propelled by everyone pulling the stick toward their chests. To reverse directions, the boatswain is suppposed to simply change gear. The propulsion then goes in the opposite direction, while the crew performs the same action. This officer couldn't figure out how to change the gear. Sensing the scorn of his shipmates when he was ordered to go in reverse, he shouted, "Okay. . .everybody up and sit the other way."

A high percentage of BC Ferries employees, both on the ships and at the terminals, holds first aid and C.P.R. certificates and an

BUILDER OR TURNCOAT ?

"As we went out the door to the crucial meeting, Bob Cook stopped and said, 'I better take a briefcase.' And we were off to settle the strike. All he had in the case was a pack of cigarettes."
—Norm Thornber, business agent (1964-1978) BC Ferry and Marine Workers' Union, referring to the 1968 strike and his colleague Cook, then representing the Canadian Merchant Service Guild.

In discussions of BC Ferries labor relations, it usually doesn't take long to get around to the name Norm Thornber and the sea of controversy left in his wake. When he talks today about the mammoth multi-year fight to build the union and all that has come thereafter, he tells the story dispassionately and with considerable pride.

No one did more than Thornber to develop the union. His name became synonymous with BC Ferries. It was, therefore, all the more startling when the tables completely reversed and he walked over to join the management bargaining team.

Social Credit, under Bill Bennett, was back in power in late 1975 and, as the years passed, tried to chip away at the extremes of the 1974 contract. Major changes were made in fares and various aspects of day-to-day operations of the ferries, including the elimination of dining rooms. All this produced turmoil within the union and Thornber found himself fighting for his professional life against a militant movement.

What Thornber describes as a "left wing" group, in a well-organized campaign and "rigged" election, won control of the union and soon fired him as business agent. He declined to move from his office until a financial settlement was reached (he refuses to confirm that the amount was $30,000). Norm Thornber was bitter and bent on revenge. He went back on the ferries in general duty, alternating between the work of a seaman and a cleaner, but the plan was to go to head office.

Thornber spent a year in the company's personnel department before becoming the Manager of Labor Relations in 1980. "It felt strange and perhaps it wasn't right, but I had the pleasure of negotiating against the group I chose not to work with."

He says he thinks he improved the contract for management and he took immense satisfaction in 1981 when the union turfed out the slate of officers who had dumped him. "Once they were gone, I was happy, and I did what I was planning to do five years prior to that—I retired," Thornber says.

A Swartz Bay crew pose after successfully attaining seamen's certificates.

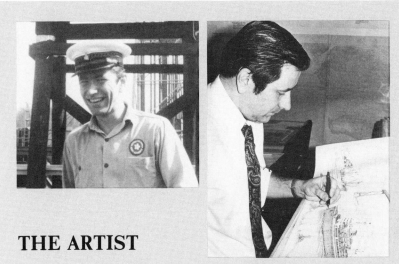

THE ARTIST

Throughout the offices of BC Ferries, and in the homes of most of the company's key personnel, past and present, visitors will find the work of Tsawwassen artist and shipping buff David O. Thorne. Few publications about the company over the years fail to use at least one of his detailed ink drawings of the ships of the fleet.

Thorne worked summers and part time as a BC Ferries seaman from 1966 until 1971, while pursuing his university degree. He taught school for a year before deciding on art as a career. Since then, he has worked full-time as an artist within the planning department of the Municipality of Delta. His ultimate dream is to one day support his young family by independently practicing his craft or, perhaps, by working professionally as an artist within the shipping industry. His work has been published in many prestigious books and magazines, including the world renowned Jane's Merchant Shipping Review.

There are many artists within the company as well. If you see a fine painting of a BC Ferry, it could be the work of Walter Wiebe of the Deas Dock paint shop, or of seamen Bill Richer, Eric Payne and Bill Hawker.

SAFETY SLIDES –
THE KAMIKAZE PIPELINE

What's faster then the speed of light? Any human hurtling down a wet BC Ferries safety slide. The fancy rubber slides, automatically ejected from aircraft, have proven to be a safe, fast and effective means of getting passengers on terra firma. It seemed, therefore, a logical progression to use the same equipment in ships. BC Ferries is never in second place when it comes to new innovations.

BF Goodrich was delighted to install the slides on the new jumbo generation of ships in the 1970s. They had tested out perfectly at the rubber company's engineering research lab. What they hadn't counted on was the effect of moisture on rubber.

When the great day for testing arrived, the company's Operations Manager, Captain Peter de Cunha, organized a complete ship's crew in their usual uniforms, and a group of head office people to play the role of passengers. It was raining. They assembled at the rail looking down the length of the snake-like slide to a distant rubber catchment raft. A small boat hovered nearby, set to gently lift survivors from the slide's base. Standing on the open deck of the huge super ferry, seeming to be as high over the water as a jumper on Lions' Gate Bridge, the testees were once again having grave doubts as to the intellect of their masters.

But into the breach went a Chinese cook, and he started merrily on his way, quickly gathering steam. With moon-sized eyes he neared the bottom, desperately clutching the sides of the slide and plummeting at the pace of a speeding bullet. He hit bottom with a jarring "ooof," bouncing off the raft yards away into the ocean. Retrieved and in shock, the cook collapsed in the lifeboat. Captain de Cunha, convinced that the first volunteer must have done something wrong, ordered the procedure to continue. Many others had the same experience, invariably ending with an undignified flip into the drink.

Captain Jimmy Bell, who was present, said, "When the ladies in panty hose went down, you could hear the smoke coming off their backsides." Chief Engineer John Rogers added, "It was like a Disneyland ride."

De Cunha, not one to ask anyone to do anything he wouldn't do, jetted down the slide in his business suit. A witness remembered, "He was the operations manager. . . .Someone yelled, 'let him drown.' " De Cunha said he wasn't pitched into the sea. "But I might as well have been. . . .There was a foot of water in the raft."

Another Chinese employee met the same fate, but made quite a fuss when they pulled him into the boat. He kept yelling, "My ankle, my ankle," but no one paid much attention. The little guy was tossed around like a sack of potatoes. Much later it was discovered that his ankle was broken.

The manufacturers and BC Ferries engineers came up with new surface coatings that improved the slides, but they were never considered satisfactory. A slide came into use only once in an actual emergency. When Queen of Alberni went aground in Active Pass, only fifteen people out of one hundred or so aboard, chose to use that exit. The slides were finally abandoned.

BC Ferries is now exploring a fabric safety chute of Japanese manufacture, said to have had great success aboard cargo ships. A passenger jumps snugly into the top of the chute, and an elevator-effect supposedly eases him gently to the water. One company executive was hardly encouraging when he described it as, "The world's largest prophylactic."

Editor Pat Stephens, and the corporate publication, The Dolphin.

extremely large number are fully qualified in Industrial First Aid. Veteran chief steward Bill Roberts says that many times people with cuts dripping blood, will bypass hospitals certain in the knowledge that an I.F.A. attendant will be aboard the ship. Sometimes people with serious problems will phone in advance requesting use of the ship's first aid room and nursing supervision during a typical crossing. "We have to refuse," Roberts said. "When it is a legitimate emergency, we do our best to deal with it, but we can't book space. Attending someone like this costs us a crew member for a whole trip."

He remembers a passenger who boarded ship in complete agony. The chap had been doing some metal work, when he caught a sliver in his backside. He went on the ferry and asked for help. Roberts guided him to the first aid station and then went to fetch a female I.F.A.

attendant. The woman emerged moments later, now apprised of the problem and accosted the chief steward, "I'm not going to be in there alone when he takes his pants down," she said.

The company has had its share of losers. Captain Jim Miller remembers a seaman who called in sick one day. The next day he was pictured in the newspaper being rescued from the sea in his overturned sailboat. Although the seaman looked relieved in the newspaper, his troubles were just beginning.

THE BROUGHTON BUNKER

Some jaded crew members refer to head office as "The Broughton Bunker," a reference to its Victoria address, with various snide comments about the company being top-heavy with management. There has been almost a deliberate effort among personnel to avoid understanding that the creation of a Crown Corporation has almost doubled executive responsibilities.

One occasionally hears from head office deprecating comments about union personnel, such as "featherbedding," in description of ship manning requirements. But as company procedures become ever more sophisticated, it is also true that managers frequently fail to see this basic flaw in their systems: if highly accomplished masters, chief engineers, chief stewards and chief cooks, are not left sufficient room to innovate and create, self-satisfaction will suffer, and with it, the morale.

Under Stu Hodgson for the company and engineer Andy McKechnie for the union, great strides have been made in recent years at improving the public image of the people within the system. A series of brochures, television ads and other promotions have displayed the many skills of the various crew members. Formal seminars have brought management and staff together for days of consultation. A slick company staff magazine, *The Dolphin,* now has several years behind it with in-house stories. As Hodgson frequently points out, "We are a team from top to bottom. . . .When I hear of morale problems, I sometimes wonder if they all realize just how good they are. . .by comparison with any fleet anywhere."

135

CATERING: A STORY OF CHINA
CHAPTER TEN

"If it had been that an applicant must be Chinese, it would be discrimination. . .but it is for a man of any race who can speak Chinese—just as a vacancy for a typist might stipulate that she had to type at a certain speed."
—Canada Manpower ruling in 1968, about complaints of discrimination in BC Ferries hiring policies for catering staff.

In every possible way, except by design, the British Columbia Ferry Corporation is a reflection of Canada's west coast—managerial development from sons of pioneers, British-born personnel from shipping predecessors, and individualistic, independently-minded political leadership from people who deliberately lacked the good sense to know their limitations. But, like British Columbia itself, BC Ferries is also a story of China.

Histories are replete with the tales of "coolie" labor in the early railway gangs, the genesis of today's Chinese society, including a Chinatown in Vancouver second only in size to San Francisco in North America. It is possible for a British Columbian Chinese to live an entire life in totally traditional ways, without ever learning a word of English.

A decision was made at BC Ferries in 1960, before the first ship sailed, to employ exclusively Chinese in the food preparation sector. Few, if any policies, look wiser under the scrutiny of historical examination. They have delivered unflagging competence, loyalty, conscientiousness and consistency. It has evolved to the point where the Chinese are a family within a family. Their society operates by its own rules, but the mutual bantering and self-confidence within the broader corporate community is a model of cosmopolitan relations.

BC Ferries is one of Canada's largest food handling concerns. It is far more than Chinese galleys. The boss in 1985 is Barry Ellett, catering manager, a chap with a successful track record of huge fast food, and department store dining outlets. The catering superintendant on the southern route, Jim Engler, was awarded "Food Executive of the Year - 1981" by the Canadian Food Executives Association, Vancouver Branch. Many other ethnic backgrounds are in key catering positions. The Chinese exclusivity on the ships has subtly diminished as the years have gone by, but examining the composition of staff today and the 25-year history, leaves only the inescapable conclusion that BC Ferries catering is, indeed, a story of China.

Monty Aldous said the catering decision was a deliberate part of his first-year obsession with winning public confidence. "I knew that no one else but Chinese would stay there and give us the kind of food we wanted. . . .They did a fantastic job under unbelievable pressure."

THE BEGINNING

Bill Lowe, the Victoria Chinese who built the catering department of the BC Ferries, says that one of the worst days of his career was when he was asked to appear at the Empress Hotel to advise a government commission about complaints M.L.A.s were receiving that the company discriminated against non-Chinese. When Lowe consulted his superiors about the obvious fact that the charges were true, it was suggested only that he find a more tactful way of telling the truth.

"I couldn't sleep at all that night," Lowe recalls. "But I told the commission that Cantonese is the language of the galleys and that we hired nothing but Chinese because they are hard workers, they don't drink and they know food."

The commission found some way out of its dilemma without altering the established policies of BC Ferries catering. Similarly in 1968, when complaints arrived at Canada Manpower, the official was to equate the need for Cantonese on the ferries to typing skills for a secretary. Whatever this was, it was not discrimination in 1968. Both Bill Lowe and the Manpower official might have a harder time satisfying today's world of complicated human rights legislation.

Company veterans remember occasions before the public services commission when Lowe and his prospective employees would assemble to determine who might be hired. Grey-flanneled government commissioners would sit before a collection of Chinese applicants. The meeting would formally be called to order. A burst of emotional Cantonese rhetoric would erupt, at the end of which, pointing his finger, Lowe would say, "Him, him and him." Decorum

Catering boss Bill Lowe's (left) Swartz Bay provisioning headquarters had undergone substantial renovation by the time this photo was taken in 1963.

Bill Lowe considers himself "employee number four" in the history of BC Ferries. *In fact, he was employee number one.* Aldous, engineer Bill Weston and political observer Ron Worley were order-in-council appointees by cabinet. There was no company until they made the first hiring decision.

Until the first ship sailed and for months thereafter, Lowe and his partner Don Eng worked out of portable trailers at the mudhole of Swartz Bay terminal. Finally, they moved their office to a small house on Michigan Street in Victoria. As the company donned more gracious apparel, Lowe was offered a secretary to do the typing. "But Don and me couldn't see much sense in having a woman around—we did the typing."

having been served, the chairman would bang his gavel and state, "Approved!"

During the fledgling early years of the company, Captain James V. Bell used to pat Bill Lowe on the back and advise, "Bill, you know, Monty, you and I are the only Canadians in this whole outfit. . . .The rest are damned Brits."

The son of a Victoria greengrocer, Bill Lowe returned to the family business in 1945 after two years overseas with the Canadian army. In 1953, he was hired by the Black Ball Line to organize the food stores and was promoted over the years to catering supervisor.

In 1960, Monty Aldous traveled to Nanaimo to visit Lowe in his storeroom. He issued the invitation to join BC Ferries in the same position and to put the food services together for the new system. "He asked me to send an application, but I didn't. I wasn't too enthused," Lowe says. But Aldous persisted, and only the overpowering offer of $475 a month clinched the deal.

THE QUICKEST WAY TO THEIR HEART—AND TEMPER

Dining has been the most controversial aspect of the ferries over the years, and many customers still long for a return to the past. Until 1976, a main routes passenger had a choice of a serve-yourself cafeteria or a table-service dining room. For the price of three dollars, you rent a spartan stateroom and have a meal delivered to you.

What became a beloved tradition to many travelers was a calculated and deliberate error from the beginning. Monty Aldous made the decision that image was the critical priority, in the face of many who were debunking the prospect of government ferries. White tablecloth service became a dining option, an expensive luxury easier to get into than out of. W.A.C. Bennett was in his best spirits when he dined aboard ship. His most regular steward at the time was Roger Carter and a little game developed between them. Bennett would ask Carter, "How do you stay so thin, Roger?" The reply, "By working for you, sir."

The dining rooms were never able to accommodate more than a small percentage of the ship's customers—cafeterias handled most of the traffic—but they required more full-time staff. Stewards not only

137

A typical galley and catering crew stand behind a portion of the popular summertime Dogwood Buffet *(top right). In his Tsawwassen Test Kitchen (below left) is Stanley Wong, BC Ferries' Quality Control Manager. With only rare exceptions, the catering staff are fully qualified seamen with appropriate safety licences.*

enjoyed the same wages as other shipmates, but they received tips. By 1976, the rooms were losing $7 million a year, but feeding only ten percent of the passengers.

The top deck dining rooms became lounge areas, except in the busy summer months, when substantial buffets are presented at meal times. At first, the cafeterias were left to handle all the year-round traffic, but Bill Bouchard, manager of communications for the company, said that it was a mistake. "People like to have a choice," he added. The solution was to create limited menu snack bars in separate areas of the ships.

In the early days, cooks had a considerable amount of freedom to prepare their own favorite dishes. Regular travelers would soon learn the specialties of each galley crew. As the years went by, with the rapid growth of the fleet and traffic volume, the charming individuality was beginning to cause problems. Food costs from ship to

138

ship varied wildly. Some cooks attracted raves and others nothing but complaints. Captain Peter de Cunha came ashore to take over the executive position of catering superintendant, with an assignment to standardize the service.

The system has become so sophisticated today that the most frequent complaint of chief cooks is that there is no individuality left at all. Everything is by the book—recipes, portions, menus and even the precise number of minutes something should be left on the grill.

THE MODERN ERA

In 1982, convinced that suppliers were frequently using BC Ferries as a dumping ground for inferior merchandise, the company decided to end it. Before this, when it was suspicious about the quality of supplies, federal and provincial inspectors were used to conduct tests. But they were inadequate. As western Canada's largest caterer and one of the most substantial customers of every supplier, it became incumbent upon the company to establish ground rules. With bold plans, a food testing kitchen was established at Tsawwassen terminal. A year later when the recession was diagnosed as an economic cancer, the fledgling operation had its budget sliced by 75 percent. But it prevailed, and a new era dawned.

Food suppliers are now regularly called to the Tsawwassen test kitchen when they wish to pitch BC Ferries on a new product line. Laboratory tests are done to determine quality and spot checks are made at all times to ensure that a supplier maintains consistency. The company's quality control manager, Stanley Wong, cooks and tests products, while salesmen stand by, nervously awaiting contracts that are rarely less than $100,000. "No one can do monkey business with BC Ferries," Wong says. Contracts have been canceled at the stroke of a pen.

The food preparation pace is relentless. A cook is shown (top right) at work in the corporate test kitchen.

139

Stanley Wong was born in Canton, the son of a man who spent a life on two continents, crossing the Pacific to relocate in the Americas and China some six times. Wong's grandfather was an original railway laborer in the last century and his father first came to British Columbia in 1910. Stanley, his six brothers and one sister were conceived during Dad's sojourns home to Canton. His father was, however, among the first group of Chinese to receive official citizenship status in Canada in 1949 and gradually much of the family assembled in this country.

Wong started with Black Ball Ferries in 1957 as a cook. When he was promoted to a relief chief cook in 1960, he was the youngest in the fleet. Bill Lowe urged him to join BC Ferries as a second cook. When Wong asked, "Why not chief cook?" He was bluntly told, "You are too young."

He came over to the government fleet with the Black Ball takeover in 1961 and remained a chief cook until 1982, when he went ashore in the executive capacity of quality control manager for the company, running the food testing kitchen at Tsawwassen and supervising the galleys at sea. Unlike many of the chief cooks in the system who have been content with their traditional ways, Stanley Wong has consistently worked at acquiring professional accreditation and qualifications, as well as proficiency in the English language. He is a member of several respected professional associations and teaches in academic institutions.

One of his first management tasks was to encourage his fellow cooks that they should view formal certification as an asset, and gradually it has come to pass. But it wasn't easy, particularly with the chief cooks senior to him in age. At first, when he would enter their galleys for a chat about procedures, he said they were very blunt, "You know the stubborn Oriental....They said, 'My boy, get out of here.' "

Wong's boss, Barry Ellett, says that the training courses are fascinating, trilingual affairs. Stanley Wong and other assisting chief cooks divide the blackboard into three sections. The first lists instructions in Chinese characters. The second display shows food items with their frequently French and European gourmet names. And, finally, in English, the blackboard shows what it really means.

The food testing kitchen at Tsawwassen terminal has produced some innovations now broadly used elsewhere. BC Ferries was one of the first large operators to feature frozen soups. The soup goes aboard ship in rock hard blocks and the cook's job is to heat and stir. As unappetizing as that may sound, the product has been a major hit. The company's traditional clam chowder is so popular its removal would provoke revolution among frequent travelers. Soup and sandwiches combine to produce 16 percent of total sales in the system. Breakfast represents 19 percent; desserts and pastries account for just 9 percent; hamburgers bring in 25 percent of the income and beverages amount to 14 percent. Surprisingly, complete hot meals, always available on the main routes, just barely climb over the 10 percent mark.

FOOD FOIBLES

A group of truckers became extremely annoyed at a regular lady customer of BC Ferries. She used to fill her purse with sugar cubes everytime she bought a cup of coffee. The truckers thought people like her put the prices up for everyone. On one occasion, a driver told her that she should stop the practice. The woman snapped back, "Mind your own business!" The truckers got together and decided to chip in on the production of a T-shirt. The deal cost them thirty dollars. One day they grandly presented the gift-wrapped package to the lady. She opened it to see a T-shirt with bold lettering, "BC FERRIES SUGAR THIEF," and the sub-heading, "How Sweet It Is!" She tossed the shirt back at them and stomped out of the room. But her thievery came to an abrupt end.

One time a lady came up with a great gimmick for stealing honey for her muffin. She'd put her honey in an empty cup, and cover it with the saucer. The muffin would be on top of the saucer. Then she'd pour a pot of tea and pay for everything but the honey. After some time had passed, the lady became so remorseful that she wrote BC Ferries to apologize, enclosing a cheque for two dollars, her estimate as to the value of the grand larceny.

The lost and found stories on BC Ferries could fill a volume by themselves. It is so routine that people leave behind valuable heirlooms and merchandise, that almost no attention is paid to it. When people are reunited with their valuables, they frequently seem genuinely surprised to discover that honesty still exists in this world. On hundreds of occasions, wallets containing large amounts of cash have been returned to their grateful owners. No one can say with absolute certainty that no BC Ferries employee has ever profited from a lost and found item, but what is certain is that cash is returned with daily consistency. Seaman Bob Swanson likely set the record in 1982 when he found a wallet containing a $2,000 negotiable bank draft, a cheque for $500 and $1,605 in cash. It was cheerfully returned to its owner.

Retired chief steward Bob Crandall probably set a record one morning on *Queen of Coquitlam* when he and his crew served 1,242 breakfasts on one 100-minute crossing from Horseshoe Bay to Departure Bay. Crandall also remembers the time when three burly loggers demanded "bear soup." The chief steward returned with a bowl full of boiling, clear water. "There you are, gentlemen, a bowl of bare soup," he said.

Definitely not the food business, but an important part of the catering revenues, has been the growth of coin-operated machines aboard the ships. With their various bleeps and other electronic noises, compounded many times by the excitement of young players, video games have been not only the rage in arcades and shopping centres, they've taken command of ferry deck space as well.

It started rather innocently. The first machines were stuck into any available open space, much like the cigarette dispensers. But instant public demand and sheer cash volume encouraged rapid expansion of the number of machines. This created sections of the ships and terminals that became noisy zoos for all those who found the devices anything but fascinating.

But by 1983, revenue surpassed $1 million annually from the video games within the system, all owned, operated and serviced by private concessionaires. But they brought a number of complaints from the majority of passengers who were seeking simply a quiet trip to their destinations. Engineers and company management went to work creating as isolated an environment for the games as possible, and the complaints have dwindled. But revenues continue to go up. The concessionaires have reported that the video business is rather fickle. There is always a new game that is the rage among the young, and the old toys fade away.

All vending machines on the ships—cigarettes, soft drinks, snacks and games—are supplied and serviced by concessionaires. The old standy-bys are the sight-seeing telescopes. Collectively, they will earn over $5,000 a month during the high season.

The company's unofficial historian is John Cass, whose experience goes back to the Black Ball days. Currently the steward for the officers mess on the live-aboard *Queen of the North*, Cass remembers a difficult problem he encountered in the early days. He would meticulously set one table in the dining room, only to return later to find the knives and forks scattered all over the table. He became convinced that one of the other stewards was playing a prank on him. He tried everything to catch the prankster, but it took a week for him to figure it out. The villain was merely ship vibration in that one section of the dining room, but only when certain propeller changes would be ordered from the bridge.

Another steward remembers spending an entire crossing locked in the linen closet. He was the last to visit the closet before the hungry passengers descended. The neurotic door swung shut behind him and automatically locked. He spent two hours banging on the door, trying to get attention, without success. His busy mates were serving their customers. Only when a steward returned at the end of a shift to get linen to reset the tables, was the chap released. His colleagues knew he was missing, but they were too busy to conduct a search.

Horseshoe Bay Terminal Agent Ken Johnson remembers his Black Ball days, and the private world of Chinese caterers. If a half dozen galley hands were on the payroll, a half dozen would be present. However, the company was convinced that there were different staff members every day. "We always had a bunch of names, and they would answer to those names. They always knew who they were supposed to be. We just were never sure who exactly they were," Johnson recalls. Black Ball also had a great deal to pay a little extra to each cook on any day the galley was short-handed, the theory being that everyone had to work a little harder. "The Chinese had it down pat. . . .They'd be one man short every day in perfect rotation," Johnson said.

Both in the Black Ball era and the early years at BC Ferries, there was always the suspicion that the Chinese, among themselves, would exchange under-the-table money to their immediate superiors, as sort of "agent's fee," for getting and maintaining the job. As the Chinese wouldn't even discuss such internal matters, the allegation was never substantiated.

Swartz Bay Terminal Agent Denny Keen found himself in hot water with the Chinese one day when he got two names confused. A cleaner thought he had won the lottery when his pay cheque arrived. Unfortunately, when a chief cook received the cleaner's pay cheque, he was not amused.

Crew rivalries and sometimes simple dislike, have led to many anecdotes. When Stanley Wong, now Quality Control Manager for the entire company, was a cook on Black Ball, he took a liking to an officer who enjoyed pork chops. When anyone else would order pork chops, including the captain, they would receive the regulation two chops. When this one officer would order, Wong dutifully put three chops on the plate. The chief steward of the ship, who despised Wong's officer pal, would instantly loom at the counter and shout, "To hell with him!" and promptly remove the third chop from the plate. This went on every day for months. Wong would put it on the plate. The boss would take it off. And, as soon as the chief disappeared, the officer would go back for a second serving of two chops. He ate four daily.

Officers' dining privileges aboard ship is a bizarre history. At the outset, BC Ferries adopted Black Ball procedures. Officers could buy their own food at 50 percent off, but the rest of the crew paid full shot

THE CHINESE ROLE EXPANDS

The most profound impact of the Chinese within BC Ferries in the future will likely come in the engineering department. There are, at this time, half a dozen Chinese second engineers, a traditional preserve of the British Isles, and most frequently, Scotland.

The first Chinese Chief Engineer was Tham Lum, who works on the jumbo "C" class ships from Horseshoe Bay to Nanaimo. A native of India and educated in marine engineering in England, he joined BC Ferries in 1966, rising to chief in 1971.

Dining facilities aboard BC Ferries ships have been a subject of public controversy from day one. Until 1976, all major vessels featured a choice of a cafeteria or a table service dining room. Severe financial losses forced changes in the system, and an end of table service, provoking public debate. Ships on major routes now offer a full cafeteria, with a broad menu, and a simpler snack bar.

The white table cloths still remain on the northern service, although patrons carry their own trays from the buffet. The photo at the immediate left displays the table setting, and, just below, the table service dining room on the main routes as it used to be.

143

or they brown-bagged their lunches. After years of protest, the company relented and passed on the benefits to the rest of the ship's company. During the early 1970s, their cost was reduced to 25 percent after strenuous negotiation. Later in the decade, the company hiked it back to 50 percent, where it remains today. Chief stewards monitor a chit system to ensure that payment is made each work shift, but over the years, company officials have watched for attempts to circumvent the system.

Cooks and crew have found many ingenious ways to pass around free food. On one occasion, head office became convinced that their policy of throwing out all sandwiches at the end of each day was starting to backfire. Some cooks made sure they created lots of extra sandwiches for their friends at home. Pressures were applied to improve galley sandwich "estimates."

Dating back to Black Ball days and continuing to the present, the Chinese have enjoyed free rice. Coffee and tea have always been free for everyone. On one ship in the early days, the chief cook would prepare a gourmet Chinese dinner for the officers once a week. The officers who wanted to partake of the repast would toss one dollar into the pot. On one occasion, ever vigilant executives expressed horror that crew were enjoying free soup. "This was really stupid," an officer remembered. "We would throw away gallons of the stuff at the end of each day."

One crew, filing an official protest, decided to do something about it. They brought a hot plate up to the bridge and a cooking rotation was established. Each day, the designated chef would bring aboard his food supplies and he would prepare a meal for all his colleagues. Bridge visitors were sometimes alarmed to find a church picnic atmosphere. Head office soon got wind of the practice and the barbecue came to an end.

A pompous British chief steward in the early days used to wear his military ribbons on his uniform. He made it clear to a German steward in his crew that he believed to be German was a disease. One day the German got the last laugh. He showed up at work festooned with his medals, neckline to waist—German military medals.

The Chinese had a tendency in early days to interpret company regulations a bit too literally. Never convinced at any time that their occidental bosses were entirely sane, they would calmly do what they were told. One day a company official came across catering superintendant Bill Lowe sitting in the storeroom surrounded by thousands of fresh eggs. He had a little scale in front of him and he was weighing eggs one at a time. Asked why he was doing this, Lowe said he received a memo from head office stating exactly how many ounces each egg should be. He was only sending to the ships the eggs that met specifications precisely.

Ron Davis, a company executive, recalls traveling on a ship one time when an irate passenger complained to a crew member. Davis asked if he could help. The chap protested that the cook had refused to make a sandwich without butter. This sounded odd, so Davis took the passenger to the chief steward and, finally, to the chief cook. As the problem was being explained to the cook, the passenger blurted, "Oh, it wasn't on this ship—it was on another one."

The Chinese contribution has grown far beyond the galleys. One cleaner of long service is the proprietor of one of the largest and most successful restaurants in Vancouver's Chinatown. Several company Chinese, with their land-based families, own thriving enterprises, working not so much for the money but to be part of a community that brings its own measure of "face" within British Columbia's Chinese society.

But the major decision that increased the visibility of the Chinese in the company was the 1976 move to eliminate the separate table-service dining rooms. Ships which may have previously carried ten cooks in two separate galleys, were reduced to five and in some cases fewer. Cooks with long seniority, under their union contract, were able to "bump" more junior employees at terminals and elsewhere. Aside from some initial language difficulties, they have successfully adapted to the new responsibilities. The galleys, however, remain dominantly Chinese, although a few non-Chinese have been able to work their way in over the years.

MOUNTAINS OF FOOD

"Our major vessels serve up to 1,000 people every two hours. . . . (They) all arrive within a 15-minute period. I do not know any other food service subjected to this type of extraordinary pressure."
—Barry J. Ellett, Manager, Catering and Passenger Services.

If one surveys the list of the top one hundred food operations in Canada, it's rare to find, among the goliaths, a firm that is not exclusively in the business. With $24 million in annual sales, BC Ferries is the largest food caterer in Western Canada, and lists at about the middle of the country's top one hundred, distributing more food than even Air Canada.

Statistics are staggering: 5,000,000 cups of coffee; 2,000,000 eggs; 420,000 donuts; 847,000 hamburgers; 380,000 pounds of french fries; 75,000 pounds of bacon; 1,000,000 bowls of soup; 2,000,000 glasses of milk and so on through the list of annual consumption. When Catering Manager Barry Ellett goes shopping for groceries, he means business.

Ellett, with a broad background in large retail and fast-food organizations, is responsible for all the revenue operations—cafeterias, newsstands, vending machines and the game arcades. The chief stewards and chief cooks report to him.

Dry cleaning and laundry statistics are equally as awesome as the food figures. A private concessionaire will do over 21,000 jackets; 64,000 pairs of trousers; 180,000 bar mops; 64,000 roller towels; 119,000 sheets and 226,000 terry towels each year on behalf of BC Ferries.

SPEED, ECONOMY AND TENSION

The most interesting time to be in a ship galley is at 3 p.m. when the crew changes. The cooks going off duty make sure every grill is full of sizzling hamburgers, the fryers are cooking chips and chicken fingers and the ovens contain the main course. They wash their hands, remove their aprons and calmly go home. They are instantly replaced by five more cooks and preparation continues as if nothing had happened. Passengers will note, however, at 3 p.m., they will wait a few minutes longer than on other sailings. The slight delay is more for the purposes of the new cash box than any time needed by the galley.

The catering staff are sensitive about criticism. The tendency of the public is to compare the food to small land-based restaurants, suffering from neither the frenzied arrival of hundreds of patrons, nor the mandate to keep prices at a minimum. Complaints about freshness are usually nonsense—everything comes aboard fresh each day and the sandwiches are made on the ships.

"I can honestly state that in twenty years of food service," says catering boss Barry Ellett, "I have not worked with a more concerned group. They have earned the right to be defended."

There have been widespread fears both within and outside of the company that financial pressures and a determination to be a no-nonsense basic transportation service will dictate a continued de-emphasis of food. The claim is vigorously denied by chairman Stuart Hodgson, who says it will always be an important part of the business on the main routes.

"If you decide to travel north of Cape Caution, there are two things you absolutely must not leave behind: your sense of adventure and your sense of humor."
—Captain James Butterfield.

Cape Caution is an outcropping of land on the British Columbia mainland coast, just north of Vancouver Island. Travel by aircraft in a slight north-westerly direction for another eight hundred miles and you will reach the point where Alaska, British Columbia and the Yukon come together. En route lies the romance, serenity and splendor of the "Inside Passage"—Grenville Channel, Princess Royal Channel, Namu, Bella Bella, Klemtu, Butedale, native villages, abandoned canneries and logging camps, and wildlife of all descriptions. The route plays host to the finest ships of the world during the summer months.

From the first sailing of *Queen of Prince Rupert* in 1966, and her more recent and spectacular partner *Queen of the North* in 1980, BC Ferries' northern masters have enjoyed genuine celebrity status throughout a part of the province too few British Columbians ever see. Tourists by the thousands enjoy the service in the summer, but, year-round, the two ships are the lifeline connecting Prince Rupert with the Queen Charlotte Islands, Bella Bella and northern Vancouver Island at Port Hardy.

"I have a personal love affair with this coast which is almost impossible to describe," says Captain James Butterfield, who has been in the northern service since 1969. He recalls going to the Pacific National Exhibition as a youngster and seeing a large model of the entire coast, complete with real water and model ships all lit up. The vision never left his memory, even through a long career on land and at sea with the Royal Canadian Navy. Retiring as a Lieutenant-Commander in 1968, he was quick to apply to BC Ferries.

It took Butterfield a while to work his way north. *Queen of Prince Rupert* was at the height of her fame and openings were few. He started on *The Salty,* the little *Saltspring Queen* serving the Gulf Islands. After his first days on the vessel, he told his wife that his ship had the best coffee shop in the fleet (there is none) and invited her to come and see it. She arrived one day and Butterfield took her below

the car deck to the engine room, spic and span with gleaming brass telegraphs and fittings. He poured her a cup of coffee from the pot on a hot plate. After a few minutes, she said, "By golly, you're right, this is pretty nice."

Over the next fourteen months, Butterfield was to serve on five different routes and on seven different ships before finally making it north in 1969. He has become a favorite in the system, conveying his love of the coast in frequent broadcasts to passengers, describing the history and significance of passing landmarks, and calling attention to eagles, seals and other wildlife. "It is still a magical thing for me to be here doing the job," he says.

The northern service is the closest BC Ferries gets to traditional passenger shipping. The officers and crews, flying in charters from the south, work for two-week stretches and live aboard the vessels. A strong sense of comraderie develops among each watch and the ships, a long way from the home base, must be largely self-sustaining. The captain is not only navigator, but director of personnel and business manager as well. Because those aboard work long days and nights, frequently up at all hours of the morning for stops at places like Bella Bella, ordinary overtime provisions throughout the fleet do not apply. In lieu of overtime, officers and crew are paid a flat 29.5 percent bonus on their base salary as a northern allowance.

Butterfield's principal ship, *Queen of the North,* is rapidly becoming the pride of the fleet, but she has had an expensive and checkered history in the service. Purchased from Danish owners for $13.9 million in 1974, *Stena Danica,* was intended to be a stop-gap attempt to deal with a serious shortage in capacity. Renamed *Queen of Surrey,* she helped relieve the burden, but the cost to renovate both the ship and the terminals for the purpose made the move questionable from the beginning. She was retired in 1976 and sat in lonely isolation at Deas Dock until it was decided to put her on the northern run in 1980.

The workhorses of the north (opposite page), Queen of the North *and* Queen of Prince Rupert *(foreground), also deliver a high standard of food and amenities.*

British Columbia's "Inside Passage" displays as fine a scenic panorama as anywhere in the world. The route hosts the finest and most expensive cruise ships each summer, but BC Ferries carries and caters to tourists at a fraction of the price.

Premier Bill Bennett is shown (top right) with Captain James Butterfield at the opening of Bear Cove Terminal. Port Hardy, in 1979.

The northern service is a different world from the bustling routes in the south. The live-aboard crews cater to passenger staterooms, cocktail lounges, gift shops and dining rooms. The terminals can be a hectic mix of effete tourists, and the rugged loggers, fishermen, miners and natives of the north.

Over $9 million was spent to make her suitable for the service, upgrading staterooms, lounges, cocktail bar and restaurants and, with her new name, she became an instant hit in the north. Extensive first class renovations were also made to *Queen of the North* in 1985, in preparation for her first season of complete dayliner service—7:30 a.m. to 10:30 p.m., one day north and the next south—offering passengers visibility for just about every inch of the spectacular route.

THE QUEEN CHARLOTTES

From a business point of view, the most controversial move the company ever made was the decision to serve the Land of the Haida—the Queen Charlotte Islands from Prince Rupert. A $5 million dock was built at Skidegate, and the route has been a big financial loser from the outset. The company's first general manager, Monty Aldous, said the decision "made absolutely no economic or political sense."

It was a by-product of the confusing year 1980. When the government decided to retire the historic *Princess Marguerite* from the successful dayliner tourist service between Seattle and Victoria, her replacement was to be *Queen of Prince Rupert,* renamed *Victoria Princess,* coupled with a jetfoil service. *Queen of the North* was outfitted to serve the north. The Seattle move proved unsuccessful and, by the fall, *Queen of Prince Rupert* was back to stay and the company had excess capacity in the north. The government was able to respond to political pressure from the Queen Charlotte Islands to provide service.

Until that point, freight and vehicle traffic to and from the islands was handled by tug, barge and other conventional cargo means. People moved back and forth in a variety of passenger craft. The highways ministry provided ferry service between the islands.

The announcement was not even universally popular in the Queen Charlottes. Many communities and native leaders expressed fears that tourists would destroy the environment and the wilderness lifestyle.

For the ship's crew, crossing Hecate Strait can frequently be torturous. While totally safe and seaworthy, *Queen of Prince Rupert* sometimes tackles seas that can rank with the North Atlantic at its worst. But sailings are sometimes canceled and the usual five-and-a-half-hour crossing occasionally takes much longer.

Until 1985, the company offered two services to the islands: the main run to Skidegate, and also a tug and barge service for trucks and cargo, berthing at Masset. The barge route lost $1 million in its last year. It was canceled in 1985. To pick up the slack, BC Ferries leased two special trucks to load and off-load drop-trailers aboard *Queen of Prince Rupert.* All traffic is routed through Skidegate.

NORTHERN TIDBITS

The northern ships are the only vessels in the system that provide cocktail lounges. With voyages of fifteen hours and more, it seemed obvious to have them installed from the beginning but it took years. W.A.C. Bennett, a legendary teetotaller, didn't even like to discuss the topic. But the bars deliver such handsome revenue that it has tempted officials to look at the rest of the fleet. It is unlikely that the government, fearing impaired driving and charges of possible complicity, could ever consider bars on the main route ferries.

BC Ferries personnel at head office and throughout the system are consistent supporters of local charities. But one of the most unique charitable efforts each year within the fleet comes from a northern service head bar steward, Joe Urbanczyk. A Vancouver tradition in every cocktail lounge in the city, through the bartenders' union, is to pass a can for the CKNW Orphans Fund and its many needy and handicapped youngsters. Urbanczyk's "Bartender's Blitz" can from the north is likely the longest distance contribution.

Rescues of stranded and shipwrecked boaters by BC Ferries in the north are so commonplace that the stories lack novelty. Most frequently the grateful boaters are brought to safety, but sometimes the ships are the first on a scene of tragedy. The two vessels have been dispatched on occasion to pick up seriously ill people in remote

JUST LIKE ESSONDALE

Many residents of the north become known to every Queen of the North *and* Queen of Prince Rupert *crew member, but none more so than a Bella Bella Indian named Josie. Many years ago, she adopted* Queen of Prince Rupert *as her own ship, never failing to greet an arrival. As the ferry personnel got to know her, they were advised by other Indians that Josie had a history of mental problems and would, upon occasion, be taken to the provincial mental hospital at Riverview for treatment.*

One day Captain Arnie Ryles took her for a tour of the ship. When Josie looked into the crew mess, she commented, "Isn't this nice—just like Essondale!" (Essondale is a mental institution in the lower mainland.) Captain Jim Butterfield confirmed the story, "In those days, it was."

On another occasion, when Josie advised she wanted to go to Prince Rupert to see her brother, the crew passed the hat to pay her return fare. Unfortunately, from that day on, she failed to understand why she couldn't always come along. She blamed the officers. One day she arrived at the ship with a huge box of baked goods announcing, "This is for the boys that does the work," making it clear the officers were to get none. Recently, Josie's photo was prominently featured on BC Ferries promotional brochures and posters for the northern service. Butterfield says, "She hasn't been the same since."

communities. On most occasions, this involves tendering to shore in small boats, gently transporting the patient back to the ship through often rough waters. BC Ferries crews have won just about every search and rescue award possible.

The public service doesn't end there. Each year in Vancouver harbor, the great cruise lines of the world often hold press parties when the Canadian Meteorological Service honors them for weather-reporting along the coast. What the international companies don't tell the media is that year after year the top-rated ships out of about 260 in the Inside Passage are those of BC Ferries.

Christmas is a grand day on all the BC Ferries ships. There is invariably a Santa Claus, carolling and general merriment. The crews are away from their families for at least the work shift, and they make the best of it. But it takes on added meaning in the north, where the crews live aboard ship for two weeks at a time. It becomes an all day party, involving passengers when at sea, and usually a great crew Christmas dinner when the passengers go ashore.

Seaman Larry Stewart became part of a strange crime story in 1982, when *Queen of Prince Rupert* was in the south getting spruced up at Deas Dock. He was making his rounds when he heard noises in the meat cooler. Convinced that it was just the ship's engineers gorging themselves, Stewart called out, "Are you guys eating again?" A voice called out that they had been sent to clean out the meat locker. When Stewart demanded identification, the culprits dropped their bulging garbage bags and took flight. As the ship's officers reported later, the attempted theft was a needless redundancy, "The engineers were already doing an effective job of cleaning out the meat cooler."

On a sailing across Hecate Strait in August 1984, Captain Dennis Hull of *Queen of Prince Rupert* ordered a seaman to fly a flag from the pole at the ship's bow. When the flag was unfolded, flying happily in the breeze was a huge white polar bear, surrounded by a blue border. The flag was in honor of the Chairman of the Board of BC Ferries, who was visiting the ship that day. The polar bear flag became the

The Chairman's special flag.

tourism symbol of the Northwest Territories when Stuart M. Hodgson was commissioner. Passing fishing boats and the residents of Skidegate must have been scratching their heads over the new flag.

A major company policy decision on the northern service in 1985 has produced consternation among the crews. They decided to hire increasing numbers of people from Prince Rupert to work on the two ships. (Prince Rupert has argued for years that it is almost shameful that *Queen of Prince Rupert,* sailing from the port since 1966, and *Queen of the North* since 1980, have had crews transported from Vancouver, Nanaimo and Victoria.)

When Kelsey Bay was the southern extremity of the northern service, the crews would be bused from Nanaimo. After the highway went through, and Port Hardy became the base, the distance was considered too great for bus travel. The company chartered aircraft. A few crew members have such an intense dislike for flying that they drive their own cars all the way to Port Hardy. Over the years, the company has tried various forms of incentives to get the crew members to move their homes to Prince Rupert, but there have been few takers. On one occasion, two employees did move their families north, believing that the others would follow. When none did, they moved back south.

Although the company plan is to base *Queen of Prince Rupert* permanently in the north, and have a total crew resident in Prince Rupert, it's unlikely to happen overnight. Corporate secretary, Al Lukinuk, said in 1985, "This is a very complicated matter. . . .No one solution will work. We will have to approach it from a number of different directions."

The officers and crew are prepared to recognize the historic injustice, but they have fully-trained licensed friends who were laid off during the recession. They ask, "Why start all over again training rookies?" The seamen propose that Prince Rupert's problem be resolved gently over time.

THE Z-DRIVE

Three vessels in the BC Ferries fleet operate with all the dexterity of motor boats. As one officer described it, "They can turn on a dime." The shaft-propeller configurations are known as "Z-drives."

When the three 50-car identical sisters Powell River Queen, Mayne Queen *and* Bowen Queen *were built for efficient service on shorter routes in 1965, the cost was about $1 million each, and their double-ended propulsion was a normal affair.* Powell River Queen *was given added space for overheight vehicles and more passenger accommodation in 1973, but the big $3 million stretching and re-engineering job was done on each of the three vessels in 1979. The Z-drives were also installed.*

The name is descriptive. The four propeller shafts protude from near each of the hull's four corners, and then probe straight down below the vessel's bottom. There are two propellers at each end. By manipulating two controls on the bridge, the captain can turn any or all of the propellers in full 360-degree circles. The maneuverability, for ferries of that size, is almost unbelievable.

The original Dogwood Princess.

THE BABY

The baby of the fleet, Dogwood Princess II, *is a 38-passenger water bus based at Langdale. She carries passengers only to and from Keats and Gambier Islands. The boat was built in 1979 to replace* Dogwood Princess, *a smaller and less satisfactory vessel.*

Dogwood Princess II *had a fast new engine installed in 1985 to bring her speed over the 20-knot mark.*

The government wharf at Bella Bella.

THE GULF ISLANDS
AND SUNSHINE COAST

An exasperated ex-manager of BC Ferries had an insight into one of the company's most persistent problems: "It is impossible to be an executive within BC Ferries for very long, before you come to the inescapable conclusion that the greatest contribution you could make to world peace would be to sink the Gulf Islands."

No matter what BC Ferries does to serve the Gulf Islands, the service is guaranteed to lose substantial amounts of money. The current daily capacity can move 6,000 vehicles to and from the islands. There are only 5,000 cars in the entire area. Salt Spring Island, with regular service between Crofton and Vesuvius, between Fulford Harbor and Swartz Bay and between Long Harbor, other islands and the mainland, must have more ferry service than any island of its size and population in the world.

But it's not enough. Residents complain. When major meetings are held to discuss ferry services, Gulf Islands residents have been known to send over one hundred different people, each claiming to represent some cove or hamlet that requires more service. The company experimented in 1983 with hovercraft. It was quick and cheap, but it didn't take cars. A few years ago, the company decided to make inter-island transport free, but shopkeepers on Mayne, Galiano and the two Pender Islands complained that all their customers were going over to Ganges to shop.

BC Ferries has to build a system knowing that the ships will be busy only Friday and Sunday nights, and then only guaranteed during the summer months. As one captain put it, "The ship could have rubber walls on a Sunday, but often we feel rather lonely through the week." Various reservation programs have been tried to cope with the weekend demand. The honor system resulted in too many "no shows." A pay in advance system started in 1985. Passengers could reserve space for the season as long as they physically paid for passage at the Vancouver Reservation Centre, or over the phone using credit cards. This brought a number of complaints. The policy was changed to permit an honor system for those booking within five days of sailing, but maintaining the pay in advance procedure for anything further ahead of time. Experience had shown that people who book close to sailing date tend to show up.

Gulf Islands people like to point out that the highways ministry ferry service to the smaller, more northerly islands, is much cheaper and almost 100 percent subsidized by government. They fail to observe that the quality of highway vessels and service is substantially less. (This is expected to change when the highways department salt water ferries are transferred to the BC Ferry Corporation at the end of 1985.)

Pressure from the Sunshine Coast and Bowen Island is similar, but their spokesmen have never been as effective a political lobby as the Gulf Islanders. There seems to be a feeling among British Columbians, that no matter how isolated a locale people choose for their homes, the taxpayer is obligated to instantly provide top flight tranportation links.

All these services lose substantial amounts of money each year, but they are a government investment that maintains the lines of communication. Financial purists who question the wisdom of the routes tend to overlook that government subsidy, usually federal, has been the story of coastal shipping in British Columbia from day one of the province's history. Canadian Pacific, Union Steamships, Canadian National, Northland Navigation and others all received the largess of mail contracts or direct hand-outs over the years.

BC Ferry Corporation is the sole survivor.

PUMPING THE BILGES: DATA & ANECDOTES

CHAPTER TWELVE

One day BC Ferries decided it was time to change the combination on all the ship safes in the fleet, a routine security precaution. Overnight, all the numbers changed and the next morning, the captains and chief stewards picked up their daily instructions, including the new combinations. One crew forgot.

As the ship sailed leisurely down romantic Long Harbor on Salt Spring Island, passengers lined up to be fed. But the chief steward was panic-stricken in his office. He couldn't get the safe open and the cashier was desperately shouting for the cash box. The mob was getting edgy. The public need for coffee and breakfast is not to be denied. The chief steward appealed to the captain on the bridge.

When the master radioed back to Long Harbor Terminal Agent Bob Anderson, he was advised that he should have picked up the new combination. The captain asked if the combination might be given to him over marine radio.

Anderson replied, "I can't do that . . . .Everyone from Prince Rupert to Vancouver will hear it."

The captain asked if he should come back, but both quickly agreed that the reprecussions would be too serious. Then, Anderson had a clever idea.

"Do you remember the old combination?" he asked. When the master said he did, the terminal agent told him to get a piece of paper.

Okay.....take the first number of the old combination, and add five," Anderson instructed.

"Got it," the captain radioed back.

"Now, go left two complete turns and subtract nine from the old number."

"Roger," comes the reply.

"Finally, go one turn back and add sixteen to the old number," Anderson advises.

There was silence for a moment before the captain jubilantly acknowledged, "Got it: 2-53-18!"

The late General George R. Pearkes, V.C., Lieutenant-Governor of British Columbia from 1960-1968, was one of BC Ferries most passionate supporters through the formative years. Few visiting international dignitaries could get out of the province before His

Honor, with limousine flags flying, would take them for a ferry ride. Pearkes, one of Canada's most renowned soldiers, had won a battery of Canadian and international medals, including a Victoria Cross at Passchendaele, during the First World War.

Monty Aldous said that Pearkes was reluctant at first to use the new ferries, but after one personally guided tour on a crossing, everything changed. "From then on, he was our greatest supporter," Aldous said.

Retired Captain Les Mollett of Salt Spring Island first sailed under Captain George Maude aboard *Cy Peck* in 1934. He remembers a regular customer known as "Two-Ton Dick Royal," who

The modern jumbos command attention wherever they appear.

would show up at the boat with massive loads that magically always weighed two tons. Over that limit, the fare went up. There were so many arguments with him that the fare structure was shifted to length of vehicle rather than weight.

One rainy, blustery day, Captain Maude had forgotten his raincoat. Face dripping with water, he appealed to his engine room oiler to borrow his coat. The oiler neglected to tell Maude that one pocket of the coat was full of graphite, conveniently placed for greasing machinery. As the day progressed, Maude would regularly remove his hand from the pocket to wipe his brow, the rain erasing any sensation of the black graphite that was spreading over his face. Passengers were terrified when Maude loomed on the bridge looking like a Welsh coal miner after a long shift.

When a ship completes unloading at a terminal, the mate on the car deck reports the fact to the captain on the bridge and then he begins loading the new cargo. When this is completed, the mate radios "all clear" to the captain and the ship sails.

One day a mate had a mental lapse. When he completed unloading, he went to the phone and he sounded the "all clear." The captain promptly ordered "slow ahead" and the ship sailed empty from the terminal. Throughout the parking lot, drivers jumped from their cars screaming in unison, "What the hell is going on?" The chagrined mate had to report his error to the bridge. The ship reversed directions and went back to load.

There are many stories of amorous couples who hide in their vehicles, convinced that the abandoned car deck will be a great place for passion once the passengers depart. Veteran seaman Hank Ward recalls a time in the Black Ball days when a loving pair were spotted at a terminal waiting line. One seaman determined to watch their activity. When the couple reached the ship, they were parked discreetly between the bulkhead and a huge lumber truck.

After confirming that the lovers had no intention of going to the lounge, and awaiting the departure of his colleagues, the seaman climbed up to the top of the truck's lumber pile. As he reached his optimum vantage point, the load shifted, and the seaman got stuck. He was reaching a stage of near panic as the ship approached Horseshoe Bay, convinced that his next stop would be Squamish. He was at first relieved to see his mates return. But, after spotting him, they prolonged the agony, making no move to help.

The rescue took place at the last possible second. The voyeur, back on the car deck, calmly brushed himself off and said, "It was all worth it."

People will try every means possible to subvert the system. There was a chap who didn't like being placed on the ferry platform decks. To avoid this, he would strap a rocking chair on the roof of his car. This worked for a while until the staff decided to have some fun at his expense. When he was told at the ticket booth that he would have to pay for an "overheight vehicle," the chair came off the roof in lightning fashion.

Stuffing extra passengers in the trunks of cars is an age-old ruse, frequently caught at the terminals or on the ships. Doubtlessly, many have gotten away with it. Horseshoe Bay Terminal Agent Ken Johnson recalls watching a blue Mercury at the end of the waiting line one day. A couple of youngsters got out of the car and climbed into the trunk. When the driver reached the toll booth, he asked how much. "With an absolutely straight face, I said that will be seven dollars for you and the car, and another four dollars for the two guys in the trunk."

Then there are the fearless ones. *Howe Sound Queen* crews remember the chap at Snug Cove, who urgently reported that he had forgotten something ashore. He asked them to take the boat back. Neatly dressed, despite T-shirt and slacks attire, he was carrying a briefcase. When the captain refused, he jumped into the water, swimming to the ladder on the dock. It was low tide. It took him yeoman's effort before a large crowd, to scramble up to the first rung.

Departure Bay crews became annoyed at a regular last-minute arrival for their sailings. The chap would quickly kiss his wife good-bye, and then dash madly for the ship, frequently jumping over a gap from the dock to the vessel as she pulled away. One day the scene was repeated, but the water expanse was broader than usual. Undeterred, he tossed his briefcase to a seaman, and adroitly made it aboard. The seaman welcomed him with a grin, "Well done sir, but we are just arriving."

One of the more intriguing BC Ferries crime stories involved Wilf Hetman, a highways department patrolman. He saw two men and a woman at Swartz Bay Ferry Terminal, drinking rather heavily. He let them board the ship, but, concerned that they might continue drinking on the ferry, he decided to report them to the police. Hetman learned that the car was wanted in connection with a bank robbery. Saanich police flew to Tsawwassen, and they arrested the culprits at the mainland terminus. Several weapons and $7,000 in cash were found in the car.

Derek Todd, a director of Victoria's Sandown Raceway, bought a chocolate bar from newsstand clerk Mary Gudmundson, while en route across the strait for races in Vancouver. He paid for the candy with a crumpled bill and received $1.60 in change. Later, a fellow passenger calmly asked him why he had paid for a chocolate bar with a $1,000 bill. Distraught, Todd charged back to the newsstand and brought the matter to Mary's attention. Equally surprised, she looked through a stack of two dollar bills in her till and came across the $1,000 note. The brown colors of the bills are similar.

With that matter rectified, Todd was premature in assuming his day would get better. A friend had given him the $1,000 to bet on a horse named "Wander Kind" in Vancouver. But, at the track, a railbird convinced him that the nag was a loser. He decided to save his pal the big investment. "Wander Kind" won easily and it cost Todd $1,500 to appease his friend.

The "midnight caper" occurred five years ago at head office. A junior clerk was assigned one night to label two boxes. In one, there was a routine batch of material for Prince Rupert. The other contained the pay cheques for everyone in the company except head office personnel. She mixed up the labels and the cheques went off in the slow bus to Prince Rupert. When the error was detected the next morning, panic ensued. The RCMP finally chased down the bus in the Fraser Canyon. Corporate Secretary, Al Lukinuk, said, "She is a delightful little girl and I'm pleased to say that she is still with us."

Pranks can come from the public, like the jock strap that fluttered from a ship's mast for a whole day before being noticed, but the best come from the crew. One mate had a favorite little game. With the toughest industrial glue he could find, he'd stick gleaming fifty-cent pieces to the metal floor of the car deck. Passengers would become positively strange in attempts to pick them up.

One day at Horseshoe Bay, Assistant Terminal Agent, Ron Cranfield, was standing at the stern of a ship talking to an officer. As the ferry started to pull from the dock, he was seized by the crew and held aboard. They were well out into the bay before Cranfield was released. Completely dressed in business suit and shoes, he dove

Moving cars the old way in the north, aboard Captain Harry Terry's Skeena Prince.

neatly into the wake.

Meanwhile, back at the terminal, a meeting was about to begin. As a newcomer entered the room, a pained official asked him, "Where the blazes is Cranfield?" The arrival responded, "He'll be here shortly. The last time I saw him he was swimming ashore!"

But the prize winning gag in company history did come from a passenger at the height of Detroit's never-ending quest for innovation. A ferry was neatly loaded one day, and a final car charged up the ramp to claim a position at the rear of the car deck. When the ship cleared the dock, the crew heard an engine start up and they were horrified to see this convertible back off the stern of the ship at high speed. They charged to the edge only to see happy faces waving from the seaborn convertible. . . .It was an "Amphi-Car," just as seaworthy as military amphibious equipment.

There was nothing happy about seaman Steve Lomax' similar experience. As a ship approached Active Pass, heading toward Victoria, Lomax also heard an engine start. He raced along the car deck just in time to see a vehicle back off into the wake. He sounded the alarm to the bridge, but could only stand in helpless horror, staring eyeball to eyeball at a man sitting behind the wheel of his floating car. Slowly, he sank to his death.

One of the old Black Ball tubs had a car deck that was so warped, efforts to wash it down were seriously affected. After the hoses were finished, a hundred mini-ponds would be left behind, some of them six inches deep. The regular routine, after deck washing, was to signal the bridge. The captain would then proceed through a series of "hard-a-ports" and "hard-a-starboards," violently wrenching the vessel until the water flooded off the deck into the sea. Passengers, clinging to their seats, rarely knew what was going on.

Terminal Superintendant, Gerry Barber, has a wealth of stories from his Black Ball days at Horseshoe Bay. Mercenary pressures from the office forced him to cram as many vehicles on each sailing as possible. One day, the last truck to board had its rear tires half protruding off the end of the vessel. Even the trucker, so anxious to get to his destination, thought it would be safe. Well into the bay, the truck, minus the driver, gently rolled off the ship and sunk into the deep. The captain reversed direction and began to return to dock. Barber said his boss ordered him to tell the captain, "Time costs money. . . .Don't come back. We'll settle with the trucker later."

When service or crew deportment don't live up to public expectations, choice words are frequently heard. But, in the reverse, ferry staff can be creative in their phraseology. The Gulf Islanders are known—not always affectionately—as "The Goofy Islanders," and Village Bay on Mayne Island has been called, "The Bay of Pigs."

When Tsawwassen was chosen by BC Ferries as a terminal, there were few in the province who knew how to pronounce the name. One still hears many variations today. John Cass, a Nanaimo historian, newspaper columnist and veteran BC Ferries steward, is also an authority on coastal nomenclature. He says the "T" must be silent.

Three ships pass at the north entrance to the tight, but scenic Active Pass (top).

The frequently heard "Tah-wassen" is incorrect. "Saw-wassen" is better, but true native dialect adds just the vaguest hint of a "T" in front of the "Saw" sound. In Cass' research, he discovered many learned documents struggling with the name: "Cheakwassen" (1857); "Chewassen" and "Tchewassan" (1878); "Cheawassen" (1920); "Tawwassan" (1945); and, "Chewassen" (1947).

BC Ferries has so many long-time active employees, that those with a mere ten years or so under their belts feel like newcomers. The senior master still at sea in 1985 is Captain John Poole. Asked if he was with the company right from the beginning, Poole replied, "No . . .I started in October. . . .I'm just a rookie." He was referring to October 1960, four months after the service was inaugurated.

One irate lady complained to Captain Paddy Hannigan that her car was wedged in too tight. Most concerned, Hannigan went to see for himself. After studying the matter, he asked the woman in all seriousness how much she had paid for her crossing. She replied that it was three dollars. "Ah," the captain replied, "that explains it. . . . This is the three-dollar space."

The many rescues, boat tows and crew exploits could form a solid base for a television series. One day, amid a near gale in Georgia Strait, a ferry crew lifted prominent T.V. weatherman Bob Fortune from his overturned sailboat. In perfect deadpan style, a crew member asked the dripping wet personality, "And who's doing the weather reports these days?"

Captain Jim Miller recalls a time when they hitched a rope to a troubled yacht, towing the sailor and his boat to Departure Bay. Once ashore, the victim said he was penniless and he had to get back to the other shore. The crew took pity on him and carried him free as they sailed back across the Strait. The passenger sat at the officers' table aboard ship and enjoyed a free meal during the crossing. The ship heard later from police that their mission-of-mercy passenger had not only stolen a car when he got off in Horseshoe Bay, he had previously stolen the yacht.

Drunken misbehavior is a cross the company has had to repeatedly endure. Occasionally well-known British Columbia sporting organizations have been banned access to BC Ferries, provoking assorted wounded protests and attempts to wield political pressure. The groups have been permitted to renew their travel only after written guarantees from prominent backers that incidents would not recur. Numerous incidents occurred in the days the company served Ocean Falls. Intoxicated loggers terrorized the ships—they would start their Vancouver leave too early in a local bar.

One day a woman was outside a ship, sitting in an exterior fender with her legs dangling over the rushing waves. She had escaped her two male friends who were found drinking heavily in a car. The ship was plowing along at almost 20 knots. Captain Norman Mains remembers that the woman was very drunk. When a seaman inched his way perilously along the rail towards her with others looking down from above, the woman, instead of appreciating her rescue, offered sexual favors at a modest price. The seaman managed to secure a lifebelt around her. When it was tugged from overhead, her blouse and brassiere were neatly hoisted off her. She remained securely on the rail.

When they finally worked her back along the fender to the car deck, a dreadful fight erupted between the woman and her two drunk men friends. Police picked them up at Swartz Bay. But Captain Mains said that wasn't the end of it. That night, a mate reported that the three drunks were back, attempting now to return to the mainland. They were transported, but a seaman stood sentry to ensure that they never left their car.

A happier story involved a little Indian boy. He was sporting a brand new watch as if it was a priceless diamond. As he played with the watch along the ship's rail, it slipped out of his hand, falling far below to a guard rail, where, miraculously, it came to rest. In tears, the little boy cried for help. It was reported to the bridge. The captain slowed to a near stop and inched the ship into the wind, the heading least likely to dislodge the watch. By now a huge crowd had gathered. A seaman worked his way along the rail. When he retrieved the watch, the passengers all erupted into spontaneous ovation.

The 25th Anniversary dinner cruise aboard Queen of the North. *Those in the photo were all with the company June 15, 1960.*

The guard rail once came into use for an escapee from the Brannon Lake Reform School on Vancouver Island. After scouting the usual island locales, police speculated that the chap may be on a ferry to the mainland. They were waiting at Horseshoe Bay. The escapee had, indeed, stowed away on the ship, but he thought he was wise to the cops. As the ship pulled in, he jumped down on the fender, climbing up the pilings when they were berthed. He was shocked to discover the police on top when he reached terminal level. Asked why he was climbing the pilings, the escapee said his small boat had flipped over. The policeman responded, "How come you're not wet?"

Social changes of the modern era have brought the company a good many construction and budget headaches. Pressures throughout society have attempted to make life less difficult for the handicapped, but ships present special problems. Safety has traditionally required all forms of ledges, ramps and ladders that turn a vessel into an obstacle course for those with physical impairments. Improving the situation has been a major modern-day expense.

Whales are frequently spotted throughout the ferry system, but rarely in so dramatic a pose (left).

There has been increasing attention in recent times to the transport of dangerous chemicals. Some chemicals that used to travel unmarked in trucks, are now prohibited by federal regulation aboard passenger vessels. Displaced truckers have caused ruckuses at ferry terminals. Special sailings are maintained on some routes for hazardous products.

The remarkable lifting of the Victoria-class ships, with a complete extra car deck, presented other problems. The lounge space did not increase as much as the car and passenger capacity. Top-deck solariums were sacrificed for more enclosed lounge seats, comfortable in all forms of weather, but when as many as 1,400 passengers are aboard, there is little space to spare. The company has struggled to keep its top-deck dining room intact for the popular summer buffets, but pressures for more lounge chairs, particularly during Expo 86, may ultimately force a removal of the serving counter and the tables. The Dogwood Buffet ($5.95 for breakfast, $6.95 for lunch and $9.95 for dinner—children under twelve, 50 percent off) accepted bank charge cards for the first time in 1985. One regular passenger likes the ambience of the dining room so much that she pays full buffet price, and then sits the entire journey sipping a cup of coffee.

Trying to provide a financial break for senior citizens has sometimes been controversial. With major fare hikes in 1976, the government instructed the company to give senior citizens 50 percent off on all sailings. This applied to passenger fare only, not vehicles. The policy was later amended to provide free passenger travel for seniors from Monday to Thursday only. Full fare is charged for weekend sailings, and at all times for cars. On the longer northern routes, seniors get one-third off on all passenger fares, on all sailings. The benefits apply only to those who can show a British Columbia Pharmacare card, held by all resident seniors. This sometimes produces complaints from visitors. The benefits are similar to deals offered seniors by other ferry systems. Alaska State Ferries, for example, allows its resident senior citizens to travel free, but only between Alaska ports—not south to Prince Rupert or Seattle.

Even the most innocuous matters can cause significant expense. After many comments from mothers that they would like to have a

First-year credibility was manager Monty Aldous' obsession in 1960. After it had been achieved, BC Ferries openly expressed its gratitude to the public (left).

Meanwhile (above), Black Bell's Smokwa *frequently required extraordinary help just to keep moving.*

FAIRY TALES

The staff news magazine of BC Ferries, The Dolphin, *is one of the slickest of its kind in the province's corporate world. Edited for the first few years by Betty Nicholson of head office and subsequently by Pat Stephens of Tsawwassen Terminal, the publication features stories about the people of the fleet, their work and their hobbies, corporate policies, ships around the world and a forum for beefs and bouquets.*

Years ago, the magazine bravely asked its readers for frank opinions about the content. One employee wrote to suggest that The Dolphin *leaned too heavily in the direction of management. Conceding that the publication could hardly become an exposé of corporate frailties, he suggested a compromise could produce "something between fairy tales and investigative reporting."*

Any independent journalistic assessment of The Dolphin *since that time would conclude that the magazine has been remarkably faithful to that definition.*

private area in which to change and nurse their babies, the company installed partitioned sections in one ladies' washroom on each ship. On the vessels which once had staterooms, there is also a separate "Mother's Room," for nursing purposes. Recently, a chief steward had to turf out an angry father and his baby. The chap insisted that he had a "right" to be there.

A more reasonable father received an instant and surprising reaction from the corporation. He articulately outlined the difficulty he had, changing his baby's diapers while kneeling on a men's washroom floor. On the basis of this one letter, the company decided to install a changing shelf in a men's room on each ship. BC Ferries is perhaps one of the few places in the world where fathers will find such

a facility. BC Ferries Communications Manager Bill Bouchard said, "It seems that we have to be first with every modern idea that comes along."

An undeclared war has existed between BC Ferries and the private boating fraternity throughout the company's history. Sport fishermen and pleasure boaters often behave as if they own the waterway, and as if the large ships were sufficiently maneuverable to navigate around them. To combat this, one of the company's most important public relations efforts in recent years has been educational visits from the Canadian Power Squadron, yacht clubs and other boating associations aboard the ship bridges.

18 1983 *Johnny Cash*

Rolf Harris

Mountbatten of Burma

Hundreds of dignitaries, from Mountbatten of Burma to Johnny Cash, have sailed aboard the fleet, but one of the most important occasions was a festive Queen of Esquimalt dinner during the Victoria constitutional conference of 1971 (top right and left). Captain John Poole and Monty Aldous share the helm with then Manitoba Premier Ed Schreyer, and W.A.C. Bennett is shown with Pierre Elliot Trudeau and Margaret.

Among W.A.C. Bennett's happiest moments involved climbing the mast of a new ship to hoist the Dogwood Fleet flag (top centre).

BC Ferries executive Ken Stratford points the way for then Governor-General of Canada, Roland Michener and Mrs. Michener (left), and, at the right, one of the company's biggest early boosters, General George R. Pearkes, VC, Lieutenant-Governor of British Columbia (1960-1968).

27th/61 *Brigitte Bardot*

One page has been stolen from a BC Ferries guest book. Jayne Mansfield, with heavy lipstick, kissed the page, and wrote to Captain Edward Cox: "To the coolest, sexiest swinger who ever moved and navigated me and the men in your and my boat . . . may I raise my glass to the mere glimpse of you!

Your . . . Jayne Mansfield. (Photocopies were saved, the original was torn from the book.)

163

INTO THE FUTURE
EPILOGUE

"We are at a historic phase. It is a very exciting challenge,"
—Lee Cochran, President of the BC Ferries and Marine Workers' Union.

Queen of Prince Rupert was making her way through the choppy waters of rain-drenched Queen Charlotte Sound in March 1985, when an officer rushed from the radio room over to Captain James Butterfield. He announced, "Lee has won it!" After a round of cheers on the ship's bridge, the captain went to the public address system and passed the word. The sounds of crew jubilation rang through the vessel. When the din died down, a visitor on the bridge calmly asked, "Lee who?. . .And what did he win?" The news was that Lee Cochran, a seaman with their northern crew since 1974, had just become president of the union.

Over the past decade there has been more turmoil within the ferry workers' union than between management and labor. First, long-time business agent Norm Thornber was dumped after a militant group took control of the executive. The new president, Shirley Matheson, yielded to widespread internal politicking in 1980 and resigned. Vice-president Andy McKechnie took over and was twice elected before Cochran's victory in 1985.

Within the union, McKechnie first gained considerable respect for helping to improve the image of the union and its membership. But as the recession led to layoffs and hundreds of disruptive seniority bumps, disenchantment grew. The majority believed that McKechnie could have done more.

Butterfield, the new president's captain for many years, says, "Lee Cochran is special. When he talks, you want to listen. There is a great deal of common sense about him."

Cochran served for eight years in the navy, retiring as a leading seaman. Returning to British Columbia, he joined BC Ferries' northern service, while simultaneously studying for the ministry in his fundamentalist church. He's been pulled in both directions ever since. At one point, BC Ferries offered him paid education leave to acquire officer's certification, but he decided to pursue religious studies. After being ordained in his church, however, he stayed at sea and soon found himself on the union executive. The former leading

Lee Cochran, a veteran seaman from both the Canadian navy and a seven-year career on BC Ferries northern routes, was elected to head the union in 1985. He sees the job as both positive, and a challenge.

seaman in the navy will soon be negotiating face to face with an admiral.

ANDY COLLIER

In 1985, when it was announced that Stu Hodgson, while retaining the chairmanship of BC Ferries, would be moving to take over bus transit and the one-billion-dollar Automated Light Rapid Transit development in Vancouver, Hodgson was determined that the change at the executive level would be smooth. Rancor and confusion had surrounded the succession from Monty Aldous to Charles Gallagher and from Gallagher to himself. He and his minister, Alex Fraser, went to see Premier Bennett with what he described as his "short list" of candidates. "Mr. Premier, my first recommendation is Andrew L. Collier. The second is Vice-Admiral A.L. Collier and my third is my friend Andy Collier," Hodgson remembers.

The news of Hodgson's impending move to transit was extremely confidential. Before the public was advised, Collier was hired. Hodgson had found him in the Bahamas where he and his wife Betty had enjoyed an extended period of blissful sailing, "I hadn't had a command at sea in twenty years so I had to buy my own," Collier said.

When he arrived in Victoria, Hodgson took him to pay a courtesy call on the premier, and then over to BC Ferries headquarters on Broughton Street. Depositing the admiral in his office, Hodgson called his staff together for an announcement. He says about fifteen people present had served in the navy. Hodgson says he advised the group that he would be remaining as chairman, but that he was moving full time to transit and that the new chief executive officer would be Andy Collier. As the erectly dignified bearing of the new president entered the room, the navy veterans came to attention. "It was vivid evidence of the respect with which Andy is held," Hodgson said. The non-navy head office staff were puzzled by their associates' actions and a tense moment followed. But from the back of the crowd, a female voice saved the day, "My God, isn't he gorgeous!" she blurted and the room erupted in laughter.

Hodgson, concerned by morale problems, particularly among the ships' officers, was delighted to have on hand a chief executive with bridge experience. At a subsequent meeting with the masters, Captain Doug Lench asked Collier what they should call him. The new president replied, "You can call me Admiral, you can call me mister or you can call me Andy—just so long as you call me."

After the applause died down, however, Collier added, "But seriously, gentlemen, what do you like to be called when you are aboard your ships?"

The captains reflected for a minute and one replied, "Point made, Admiral."

And Collier advised them that day, "The difference between a pat on the back and a kick in the backside is precisely twelve inches."

Passengers find many ways to amuse themselves aboard ship. Some seek only serenity.

THE ADMIRAL

"Andy Collier still believes that his D.S.C. came as a result of his magnificent performance as a navigator. . . .But it is just possible that this expedition would not have started when it did had it not been for the fact that he had stepped into my cabin and inspired me with courage at just the right psychological moment."—Jeffry V. Brock, R/Adm. (ret.) RCN.

Andy Collier grew up in the British Columbia interior town of Salmon Arm, dreaming from the age of twelve about one day joining the navy. Upon graduation from the Royal Canadian Naval College, Royal Roads, he began what was to be one of Canada's most distinguished military careers.

He was Chief Staff Officer to then Captain (subsequently, Rear Admiral) Jeffry V. Brock aboard the tribal class destroyer HMCS Cayuga one dark, dreary night in December 1950, when desperate word reached the ship that the Americans were in retreat and under heavy bombardment, without any cover. Between Cayuga and Chinnampo, Korea, was a narrow, mine-infested channel. Brock, in command of several destroyers, told Collier to navigate. Despite Cayuga's accurate lead, two of the ships would run aground in the muddy riverbed and, once freed, would have to withdraw. The mission was a major success and Lieutenant Andy Collier was awarded the Distinguished Service Cross.

His career would take him through the command of both Esquimalt and Halifax, a posting as naval attache at the Canadian embassy in Washington, D.C., and, finally, as Vice-Admiral, the principal naval officer in the country. He has vivid recollections of his years in Watergate-era Washington. "It was awkward for those of us in the foreign community. All of our American friends were very embarrassed about the entire affair and the whole city was abuzz," he said.

In 1980, Collier retired from the navy to begin a four-year term as Commissioner of the Coast Guard. When he felt his job was done and that service was in good shape, he decided to fulfil a dream. He and his wife bought a boat, moved to the Bahamas and went sailing. "Betty proved to be an excellent navigator," he said. A call from British Columbia was to prematurely end the idyllic sojourn.

SUPER, NATURAL *British Columbia offers so many vistas, that photo contests are conducted with a degree of peril—entries are overwhelming in both quantity and quality.*

In conjunction with the publication of this book, a contest was conducted offering prizes in a variety of categories. The sunset (left), taken from a ferry by Clint Kittle of Victoria, was one of the winners.

When his friend from years past, Stu Hodgson, tracked him down in the Bahamas, Collier wasn't at all ready to end the sailing, but a return to Victoria was in the cards for the future. After his command at Esquimalt had ended in 1977, the Colliers kept their Victoria home, renting it out. "My hope was to retire there and perhaps find some useful work. Usually those two things are mutually exclusive." The BC Ferries offer, while premature, seemed to fill the bill.

"This is an opportunity for me to do something for British Columbia," he said. He says he has been most impressed by the people he has met thoughout the system.

The major wild card in corporate planning during 1985 has been the prospect of Expo 86. A record year is anticipated and everyone and every ship should be in service. But the company cannot afford to implement expensive services for Expo if it means they will become a redundant part of overhead in the years that follow.

The first solid signs of economic recovery have surfaced in 1985. Major problems accommodating truck traffic between Horseshoe Bay and Departure Bay occurred during the winter months. The vehicles were carrying hard goods for the retail trade, the best indicator that people again have money to spend.

The salt water fleet of the provincial highways department was transferred to the BC Ferry Corporation at the end of 1985, adding about twelve vessels to the system. These include one large ship, *Princess of Vancouver,* the former CP vessel that has been serving Comox and Powell River, and a return to BC Ferries of *North Island Princess.* But most of these boats are small. It is unknown at this time whether all of these routes and vessels will continue in their present service, or whether better BC Ferry ships—excess to current capacity needs—may be transferred elsewhere. The company faces the task of absorbing 400 highways department employees into its own payroll, and the establishment of management offices in several new terminal locales. Highways Minister Fraser said that appropriate increases in BC Ferry Corporation subsidies will be transferred with the ships.

The expansion has come at a time when BC Ferries had more ships and crew than it needs, but until the Expo anomaly is absorbed,

no capacity decisions can be made.

BC Ferries is not resting on its laurels. *Queen of the North* received a $500,000 facelift during 1985 and she was proudly put on display in Vancouver and Victoria before beginning a northern dayliner service on June 1. Fancy new gift shops are being built for all the major ships, carrying a much broader array of merchandise than their predecessors. Chairman Stu Hodgson said that when the first of these appeared on the ships, giftware revenues tripled overnight. The former space occupied by the newstands are now "Game Rooms," confining the activity and noise away from passengers who enjoy peaceful cruises. "People want to do something—only a few are bookworms," he said.

Hodgson sees a future where passengers, not cars, will dominate strategic planning. "It has always puzzled me why we have to get the cars as close to the ships as possible, but put the foot passengers so far away." He expects to see a day when there are no buses at all on the ferries—buses will drop people off and pick them up at each end.

When gas, cars and the ferry fares were all inexpensive, there were few foot passengers. The pressure was vehicular and to maintain fast ship turnarounds, terminal design reflected the demand. Yet the chairman says that the federal license of the ships is based exclusively on a crew-passenger ratio, "They don't care if we carry a million cars."

BC Ferries engineers have been struggling in recent times with a bold plan to convert the fleet to burn compressed natural gas. Diesel fuel is now costing the company $30 million a year and the future projections are for ever-increasing prices. British Columbia enjoys tremendous reserves of natural gas, and an Australian ship, *Accolade II,* has demonstrated for three years that C.N.G. can be safe and economical. When BC Ferries first approached the Canadian Coast Guard with a proposal to use *Queen of Alberni* as a pilot project, the inspectors, at first, balked. Subsequent meetings won approval to experiment with either *Queen of Alberni* or *Queen of Vancouver,* and for BC Ferries to build a fueling compressor station at the spacious Tsawwassen terminal.

The original company cost estimates were $35 million to convert the entire fleet, an exciting prospect in the face of a 1985-dollar cash saving of $10 million per year—a third of the $30 million annual fuel bill. But the latest information has indicated that horsepower efficiencies, ultimate speed of the ships, and schedule predictability for the public has once again put the plan into the arena of cautious study.

Premier Bill Bennett says the recent transfer of salt water highways department vessels to the ferry corporation is simply a sensible consolidation in the face of government policies to phase out highways department interior ferries as other construction projects take place. "The salt water service will never be replaced by a bridge," he said.

But the premier states a commitment to keep the BC Ferries system as fine as any in the world. "The dramatic days are over. It is now a very sophisticated operation, with an ability to plan and to more ably and predictably carry out those plans."

Gift shops and newsstands have changed many times over the years, from small to large, and when space was considered more valuable for other purposes, they would be shrunk again. An early cubby hole (centre) on Queen of Victoria, *and the fancy new shops (top) appearing on the fleet in 1985.*

TABLE OF SHIPS

(Note: At this writing, the British Columbia Ferry Corporation was in the process of absorbing the salt water service of the Ministry of Transport and Highways. Most of these are small vessels, but the fleet also includes the substantial former CP ferry *Princess of Vancouver* and a return to BC Ferries of *North Island Princess*. The following table lists all the vessels that have served the company during its first twenty-five years: June 15, 1960 - June 15, 1985.)

** Asterisks denote vessels no longer in the BC Ferries fleet on June 15, 1985.

Queen of Sidney & Queen of Tsawwassen

The originals of the BC Ferry system, commissioned at the height of political controversy, the ships continue to serve the market in 1985. Shortly after sailing in 1960, dining rooms were added to the main decks. In 1971, platforms were added to the car decks increasing capacity from 106 to 138 cars. They are otherwise unchanged. Built at a cost of $3.5 million each, and originally named *M.V. Sidney* and *M.V. Tsawwassen*, these vessels set the standard for the company.

Gulf Islands Ferries was purchased by BC Ferries September 1, 1961. The vessels and terminals came as a package for $249,823.

**M.V. Cy Peck

Built at Tacoma, Washington, in 1913, she sailed first as *Daily* and came later to British Columbia to join the Canadian Pacific fleet as *Island Princess*. She was sold to private interests in 1930 who founded Gulf Islands Ferries. Renamed in honor of a local war hero, the 18-car, 135-passenger *Cy Peck* would serve until sold by BC Ferries for $5,000 in 1966.

**M.V. George S. Pearson

Originally named *Wollochet* and *Fox Island* in Washington State, the 18-car vessel came from Gulf Ferries and served BC Ferries until sold for $15,000 in 1966 to owners who wanted to use her as a fish camp.

**M.V. Pender Queen

CP's first purpose-built diesel-powered auto ferry, the wooden-hulled, 40-car, *Motor Princess* first sailed in 1923. She was originally built for $240,000. She was retired by BC Ferries in 1980 and sold for $75,300 in 1981 to a Salt Spring Island company.

M.V. Saltspring Queen & M.V. Vesuvius Queen

The nearly identical sisters came to BC Ferries from different directions. *The Salty,* formerly named *Delta Princess* had crossed the Fraser River before the Deas Tunnel was built. She was in the Gulf Ferries fleet at the time of the takeover. But her sister, *Lloyd Jones,* was in Kelowna until the floating bridge made her unnecessary. Cut into pieces, she was transported back to the coast. First named *Bowen Queen* and subsequently *Vesuvius Queen,* she has served several of the short island routes. The two 36-car ferries continue in service and feature beautiful, gleaming brass bridge and engine room fixtures.

The Black Ball Line—ships and terminals—was acquired immediately following the Gulf Islands takeover in the fall of 1961 for a package price of $6.7 million.

**M.V. Jervis Queen

Originally named *Bainbridge,* the 45-car, 600-passenger double-ended vessel was built in Houghton, Washington in 1928. She came to B.C. with Black Ball in the 1950s, before being sold to BC Ferries and renamed. She was retired from service in 1966 and could be seen rotting at a Fraser River pier along River Road in 1985.

**M.V. Langdale Queen

One of the greatest ships ever to grace British Columbia waters, she was launched in Philadelphia in 1903 as *Asbury Park*. Her service took her to New York, San Francisco (named *City of Sacramento*) and Washington State (named *Kahloke*). As *Kahloke* for Black Ball and *Langdale Queen* for BC Ferries, the 80-car vessel with stately passenger amenities principally served the Langdale and Horseshoe Bay route. She was retired in May, 1977.

**M.V. Quillayute

The first of the Black Ball ferries to be dumped by BC Ferries, *Quillayute* had a capacity of 35 cars and 600 passengers. Sold in 1963 for $9,000, she was to end her days as *Samson IV,* billed as "the handsomest fishing camp on the coast."

**M.V. Sechelt Queen

The most modern of the Black Ball Line, *M.V. Chinook II* had been built in Seattle in 1947. The 83-car, 670-passenger vessel served BC Ferries until 1976 when she was given to the Ministry of Transportation and Highways for the Comox-Powell River service.

**S.S. Smokwa

The Smokey was the last steam-engined ferry on the North American west coast. In many ways, she was a mechanical nightmare. Originally built in 1946 in Nova Scotia, she crossed Halifax harbor known as *Scotian*. She was towed through Panama and up the west coast by Black Ball. BC Ferries was quick to retire her.

Queen of Victoria & Queen of Vancouver

Construction of *M.V. City of Victoria* and *M.V. City of Vancouver* was ordered in 1961 before the cheering had stopped for the first new ships of BC Ferries. Launched in 1962, the sisters had a 106-car capacity, similar to *Sidney* and *Tsawwassen,* but they differed in many cosmetic ways. The most important alterations were less satisfactory engines and a broader-beamed car deck capable of future expansion. Originally built for $3.5 million, the installation of platforms increased car capacity to 150 at a cost of $146,500 in 1968. During 1970, 84-foot midsections were welded in place at a cost of $2.5 million, but the largest investment was "lifting"—inserting an entire new car deck—in 1981. This cost $11.3 million per ship. Car capacity increased to 284.

Queen of Esquimalt & Queen of Saanich

These ships sailed a year after *The Vic* and *The Van.* Their construction history and costs have been virtually identical. In the modern-day stretched and lifted configuration, *Esquimalt* and *Saanich* can carry up to 400 cars. They are no larger than their two big sisters, but they have complete platform deck space for extra automobiles.

Queen of the Islands

Still technically part of the fleet, *Queen of the Islands* has not been active in recent years. Constructed by Burrard Dry Dock in 1963 from a Quebec design, the 40-car, 483-passenger ferry was built to open the mainland to the Salt Spring Island route. She was to cause mechanical problems throughout her days, and the car deck was difficult to load. She cost $2.1 million in 1963.

TABLE OF SHIPS

Queen of Nanaimo, Queen of New Westminster and *Queen of Burnaby*

The final three of the original generation of major BC Ferries ships sailed first in 1964 and 1965. They are replicas of *Saanich* and *Esquimalt,* but they are powered by the same Mirrlees Twin engines that were successful on the first two ships of the fleet. The three have had platform decks installed and they have been stretched, but they have not, to date, been lifted. Their capacity remains at 192 cars.

Bowen Queen & Mayne Queen

Initially built in 1965 as 50-car ferries for islands service, these two vessels were stretched to a 70-car capacity in 1979. At the time of the stretching, a Z-drive engine and propeller system was installed. Two props at each end of the boat are maneuvered from the bridge with precisely the same effect as an outboard on a speed boat. They cost $1 million each to build, but the 1979 reconstruction cost $3 million per vessel.

Powell River Queen

Once identical to *Bowen Queen* and *Mayne Queen, Powell River Queen,* had her superstructure lifted in a $3 million 1973 undertaking, creating more capacity for overheight vehicles. At the same time, her passenger cabin was expanded. She received an additional $3 million work for new engines and stretching in 1979.

Queen of Prince Rupert

It was a great occasion for W.A.C. Bennett in 1966 when service opened to the north with a vessel that had it all—staterooms, cabins, recreational amenities. *Queen of Prince Rupert* was to be the flagship of the fleet until the honor shifted to *Queen of the North* in 1985. A Danish design, she was built at Victoria Machinery Depot for $6 million. The 5,800 gross ton semi-cruise ship can carry 80 cars, 458 passengers and a live-aboard crew.

**M.V. Sunshine Coast Queen*

The *Susy Q* had a checkered life before arriving in British Columbia in 1967. Built in Michigan in 1951, she sailed as *Jack Dalton* and *Vacationland.* A heavy semi-icebreaker, she was sold to Quebec where she crossed the St. Lawrence as *Pere Nouvel.* When she was offered for sale in 1967, the 172-car ferry was too attractive a deal to pass up. BC Ferries sent a crew east and they took the ship through Panama and up the coast to local waters. *Sunshine Coast Queen* was the first large "double-ender"—a ship with a bridge and propeller assembly at each end to avoid having to turn around at the docks—in the fleet. She was a familiar landmark until she was retired in 1976 and sold for $1.3 million in 1981. Through all her days, the extreme icebreaking weight made her an expensive ship to operate.

BC Ferries bought two of Sparky New's Coast Ferries vessels on June 1, 1969, taking over service from Brentwood to Mill Bay, and on northern Vancouver Island.

**M.V. Island Princess*

For most of her days with BC Ferries, *North Island Princess* connected the end of asphalt at Kelsey Bay, with Beaver Cove, near Port Hardy. The route also served the island communities of Alert Bay and Sointula. When the highway was finally completed in 1979, she became redundant, and she was transferred to the Ministry of Highways for service between Powell River and Texada Island. Built in 1958, she was an awkward little vessel with four staterooms and a car capacity of 20. In 1971, BC Ferries stretched and widened her, converting the hull into a catamaran. She is to return to the BC Ferries family at the end of 1985, with the elimination of Highways Department salt water ferry service.

M.V. Mill Bay

The only vessel in the BC Ferries fleet without radar, little *Mill Bay* has plied back and forth across Brentwood Bay since she was built in 1956. She has a 16-car capacity. Her future, and that of the Brentwood—Mill Bay route, is a perpetual source of speculation.

**Dogwood Princess & Dogwood Princess II

The little guy joined the fleet in 1969, a 31-foot, 30-passenger water taxi to ferry people and not cars from Langdale to Keats and Gambier Islands. She was replaced by the larger, fancier and faster *Dogwood Princess II* in 1979. She carries 38 passengers.

M.V. Howe Sound Queen

BC Ferries acquired *Napoleon L.* from Quebec in 1971 for $350,000. The 70-car, 330-passenger vessel shuttles between Snug Cove on Bowen Island and Horseshoe Bay.

Queen of the North

Freshly refurbished once again in 1985, *Queen of the North* has become the flagship of the BC Ferries fleet. The cruise ship car ferry was built in Germany in 1969 for Danish owners and christened *Stena Danica*. Purchased for $13.8 million by BC Ferries in 1974, she was rushed into service as *Queen of Surrey* to help resolve a serious shortage of ship capacity. After new ships better suited for the ferry routes entered service in the mid-1970s, she was to spend an ignominious period of years at Deas Dock awaiting a decision as to her future. Over $10 million was spent to prepare her for her days as *Queen of the North*. She features a car capacity of 157, staterooms, recreational, dining and assorted amenities. The 1985 work cost an additional $500,000. She also has a live-aboard crew.

Queen of Cowichan & Queen of Coquitlam

The first of the jumbo 360-car double-ended super ferries, the $20 million ships launched a new era for BC Ferries in 1976. Escalators and elevators connect the car decks with the broad expanse of lounge and cafeteria areas. They cost approximately $20 million each to build.

Queen of Alberni

Built at the same time as the first two jumbos, *Alberni* was designed to carry predominantly overheight vehicles. Her hull, engine and technical configurations were identical to *Cowichan* and *Coquitlam,* but her vehicle deck was a vast open cavern suitable for 58 semi-trailers or 145 cars. She also had substantially smaller lounge areas. Her original cost was about $17 million, but $9 million was spent in 1984 installing an extra 150-car deck. Lounge areas remain smaller than the other jumbos.

Queen of Oak Bay & Queen of Surrey

Substantially the same as *Cowichan* and *Coquitlam,* the latest two giant double-enders were added in 1981. The construction price had risen to $23.8 million. From the exterior, the most obvious difference is that the bows of the two ships are much more snubbed than the leaner lines of the first two jumbos. This was done for greater ease in berthing. The escalators, which had caused a number of mechanical problems and some passenger accidents on the first two ships of the generation, were deleted. Elevators serve the handicapped.

PHOTO CREDITS

Allen Aerial Photos Ltd.: 49, 50, 51 (bottom).

Bannerman, Patricia: 57, 72 (left), 93, 138 (bottom left), 139 (top right), 142 and 152 (top right).

Barber, Jeff: 13, 16, 17 (bottom), 19, 82 (top), 83, 85 (top left), 126 (top left), 127 (bottom), 135 (right), 143 (top right), 145, 149, 169 (top), 119, 120.

Benn, Don: 169 (bottom).

Brogren, Klas: 25.

Chapman, Len: 38 (top)

Ciccone, Vern: 107

Commercial Illustrators Ltd.: 47, 67.

Croucher, Gordon: 109.

De Visser, J.: 122.

Frith, Joe: 165 (top).

Galbraith, Jim: 44 (top), 71 (third from top).

Halbett, Bill: 110.

Harrison, Luke: 42 (lower left and right).

Jennings, B.C.: 10, 20, 21 ,22, 58 (bottom), 59 (bottom), 60, 61, 74, 75, 76 (right), 78, 127 (top left), 131 (top left), 139 (top left), 139 (bottom), 143, 148 (top left and top centre), 149, 159 (right).

King, Lily Lee: 27, 161.

Kittle, Clint: 167.

Landry, Patricia: 124.

LeBlanc, Don (Croton Studio): 68, 76 (left), 80, 163 (bottom).

Lund, John: 114 (bottom), 115.

Mason, Ross: 137 (left).

McDonald, Cim: 91.

McKain, Ian: 72 (right), 103 (top).

Morrison, John: 169 (centre right).

Old Masters Studio: 164.

Ryan, Jim: 52, 53, 46, 64, 65 (top left), 66, 70, 101, 103 (bottom), 154, 155, 162 (top centre).

Simpson's Studio: 82 (bottom).

Stablyk, Brian: 2.

Stephens, Pat: 133 (left).

Svendsen, Jorgen V.: 56.

Whittaker, Gordon: 162 (top left), 163 (top).

Williams, Kate: 138 (top).

Winn's Photography: 44 (bottom).

Winter, David: 165 (bottom).

Yunge-Batemen, Nick: 17 (top).

Other photos courtesy of British Columbia Ferry Corporation, Vancouver City Archives, Legislative Library of B.C., Image Bank (Tourism B.C.), British Columbia Provincial Archives, *North Island Gazette* (Port Hardy), San Francisco Maritime Museum, David O. Thorne, *Deta Optimist,* W. Kaye Lamb, Richard Mouat Toynbee, Frank A. Clapp.

Pages 37 (top right) and 39 (bottom) courtesy of George Bayless, co-author of *Ferry Boats: A Legend on Puget Sound.*

Cartoons by Len Norris, the *Vancouver Sun.*

Drawings, David O. Thorne.

BIBLIOGRAPHY

British Columbia Ferry Corporation. Numerous reports, documents and archival material, Victoria.

Brock, Jeffry V. *The Dark Broad Seas, Vol. I,* Toronto: McClelland & Stewart, 1981.

Cadieux & Griffiths, Garth. *The Dogwood Fleet,* Victoria: Cadieux & Griffiths, 1967.

Clapp, Frank A. *Inland and Coastal Ferries,* Victoria: Ministry of Transportation and Highways, 1981.

Clapp, Frank A. Articles from *Steamboat Bill,* Chatham, N.J., and other publications.

Ford's Travel Guides. *Ford's International Cruise Guide,* spring 1985 edition, Woodland Hills, CA.

Hacking, Norman & Lamb, W. Kaye. *The Princess Story,* Vancouver: Mitchell Press, 1974.

MacPherson, Ken & Burgess, John. *The Ships of Canada's Naval Forces 1910-1981,* Toronto Collins Publishers, 1981.

Plus 2 Ferry Consultation. *Ferry and Ro-Ro Guide 1982,*   Halmstad, Sweden.

Rushton, Gerald A. *Whistle Up The Inlet,* Vancouver: J.J. Douglas and Co., 1974.

INDEX

INDEX